MW01199420

THE ETHICS AND PASSIONS
OF DRESSAGE

THE
ETHICS
AND
PASSIONS
OF
DRESSAGE

CHARLES DE KUNFFY

Half Halt Press
Middletown, Maryland

The Ethics and Passions of Dressage

© 1993 by Charles de Kunffy

Published in the United States of America by

Half Halt Press, Inc.
6416 Burkittsville Road
Middletown, MD 21769

Designed by Clara Graves

Photo credits: Charles de Kunffy, Richard F. Williams

De Kunffy, Charles
  The ethics and passions of dressage / Charles de Kunffy.
    p.   cm.
    ISBN 0-939481-33-2 : $19.95
    1. Dressage   2. Dressage—Philosophy.   I. Title.
  SF309.5.D444 1993
  798.2'3—dc20   93-33153
                                                        CIP

Contents

Foreword

This book is my most personal. I have allowed myself to feel no compulsion to write yet more about riding and training skills. The rider's state of mind, emotions and character are all more important to horsemanship than are specific skills.

This book is written much like a personal letter. Its intimacy comes from the best questions that riders asked. It was improved by good editorial help from Mr. Ivan Bezugloff, Ms. Elizabeth Carnes and Mr. Richard Williams. Ivan put some of these thoughts in front of a reading public first. Elizabeth honored me by publishing it. Richard helped me sweep the cobwebs out of the corners of my thoughts.

The illustrations consist of artistic renderings of horse and rider, photographed by the author and Mr. Richard Williams. Where the mind travels, the body eventually goes to visit. The wonderful technology of cameras have preserved the memories of inspiring art. While contemplating equestrian art, some of the most proper thoughts occur.

Prologue

The art of riding is a Baroque art. The ideology is based on the Baroque view that the potential of random nature remains unfulfilled until man elevates it by cultivated design to the level of art. The ultimate equestrian goal of developing every horse's genetic potential to the fullest extent is in absolute agreement with the Baroque commitment to elevate nature's creatures to be living monuments of art. Therefore, the "modern rebirth" of the equestrian arts, as well as its last major innovations, rest in the Baroque Age. The exceptions to this are the much more recent and revolutionary innovations in the field of jumping.

The basic schooling philosophy of riding is rooted in the Baroque "World View" (or *Weltanschauung*). There are two basic commitments for riders, both of them born of our love and respect for the horse. One of these is to rebalance the horse under the added weight of his rider and his equipment. This is a never-ending process that remains at the heart of a young horse's training. Later, when the horse's strength is increased and his skills multiply, the balancing of the horse costs his rider less effort and concentration. However, the perfecting of the composite balance of horse and rider is a never-ending task.

Beyond the reestablishing of the horse's natural balance and the resulting clarity of his gaits under his rider, there is still a larger commitment. Nothing less is called for than the human genius to develop an aesthetic living, moving monument borne out of his horse's natural, inborn gifts and abilities.

Baroque man believed that nature is a wonderful treasure of raw potential. However, nature can be elevated to art only by the intervention of man. By itself, nature can never amount to art because it is random. Nature also lacks self consciousness, self awareness, with the exception of humans. Those with religious beliefs interpreted man's self awareness, his insight into his own potential, his will to create change and his ability to change nature around him, as the many signs of God's will to invest humans with creative powers. The human ability to create by willing change is his closest resemblance to God, the creator.

Those not of religious bent and beliefs, however, still recognized the unique human predicament created by self awareness and human consciousness of existence and mortality. Only through human awareness and insight into nature's potential was born the transcendental need for order and design. The human craving for aesthetic beauty animated mankind to address random nature and transform it into art. By pruning, planning, designing, rearranging, ordering, organizing, hybridizing, trimming, nurturing, altering and grooming, man willed nature to be elevated to art. It is the very essence of "humanness," the distinguishing and definitive character of people having insight into nature, a sense of order and altering by purpose of design that which is chaotic and random.

The beauty in art is a celebration of man-made order by design. Nature is art's raw material. Art is invested with human imagination, a longing for beauty, with ecstasy in understanding, the thrill of intelligent planning and a profound sense of fulfillment when something new is born.

Riding is, again, a Baroque art, with the goal to develop all the natural, inborn talents of each individual horse. The horse, a creature through which nature manifests itself, does not volunteer to elevate himself to become an object of art. Horses have no insight into their own latent potential. They lack consciousness. Complex intellect for abstract thinking, ability to reason, analyze and synthesize are not part of equine nature. Horses cannot plan the fulfillment of their own potential. They are not even consciously aware of what they might be.

Horses will not voluntarily become monuments of art. They do, however, passively await the guidance of their rider and the nourishing, nurturing, and honing of their talents. Indeed, when all of their talents are developed and are on display, they become a living monument of art. Exquisite horsemanship allows the human genius to ennoble nature by design and elevate its creature, the horse, to living art.

Baroque art with its swirling, elaborate, animated, yet ordered turbulence, comes to its finest fulfillment when a fully schooled horse is allowed to display his beauty. Curvilinear, rotund, magnificently excessive in exuberance, a fine-moving horse may have no peer in Baroque imagery, save grand opera, where the music and singing aim to maximize the drama and the intensity of emotions for the audience. Baroque means irregular, grotesque, and its symbol is the irregularly shaped pearl. Indeed, the rotund definition of perimeters of an irregular but extravagantly baroque pearl with its excessive beauty and opalescence elusiveness of color stands to symbolize Baroque achievement.

There are aesthetic pleasures prompted by various standards of beauty. Proportion, order, tempering of excess, could be such standards but these are not the ideals of Baroque. In contrast to Baroque ideals, the contemporary "World View" emphasizes that change is good and represents progress. A high value is placed on expediency. Innovation with invention in mind is valued. Technological solutions to problems are sought. Ambition and promotion of the individual's ego and a desire for public attention are forces that animate people. In contrast to our contemporary cultural style, Baroque wants beauty including energetic, excessive, turbulent, opulent, gorgeous imagery. Moving in all directions, in many dimensions, swirling from a heady abundance of energy, its only perimeters were imposed by human endurance for excessive emotional turbulence. The taming of equine exuberance of energy into a magnificent display of orderly energy is an opulent example of the very definition of Baroque aesthetic and ideals.

Extravagance, attention to detail and ornamentation always add rather than detract from the Baroque conception of perfection. The grand design is always the result of beautiful and carefully executed minutia. The stunning precision of seemingly frivolous detail has the cumulative affect a perfection through grandeur. Therefore we remember that the "finished horse" is born of daily attention to minutia in schooling. Careful consistency, repetition and elaboration are part of that daily work which produce the supple horse. The Baroque capacity to integrate complex movements and exquisite detail into a sweeping rhythm of design has its magnificent activity which allowed any space to be filled with its three dimensional presence.

The rider, the "human genius" that refines random nature into an edifice, is the ultimate beneficiary of this art. Provided he understands his horses well, the rider will have created beauty that is the physical aesthetic manifestation of his intellectual understanding and spiritual depth. So can man be elevated by the taming of his horse, through a partnership with him, to become himself the object and the subject of his art.

1
Attention to the Tradition of Classical Horsemanship

Whenever I teach or judge, I look for the same basic qualities in well-gymnasticized horses. Regardless of their level of training and athletic development, all horses should be relaxed. They should move with an elastic musculature that propels supple joints. Elastic musculature is a more sophisticated sign of relaxation than is mere absence of tension. Supple joints are strong; strength promotes supple use. Only horses that are elastic and supple can move with engagement in the haunches and lightness in the forehand. The goal is self-carriage under the rider's weight. Thus any horse, depending on his level of gymnastic achievement and athletic development, should "carry himself," rather than merely move (or worse, run) forward.

When I observe parts in a horse's body which are not relaxed, where movement appears to have been blocked, I know that the horse is neither supple nor elastic and is, to some degree, incorrectly trained. A horse "held in shape" by his rider is only posturing in a seemingly correct form, usually for the benefit of inexperienced observers. Good riders only want form which results from correct gymnastic content. They understand that one cannot shape a horse, only his energy. Therefore, to know both how to energize, and, having created energy, how to control it for the benefit of the horse, is the true science of horsemanship.

Energy should permeate the horse in his entirety. Movement should transfuse the whole horse. The energy of the haunches should penetrate through to the whole physique of

The soldier is confident, enthroned on his horse. An exemplary seat on a proud horse. Both keenly observing different things, yet obviously aware of each other and suggesting to the observer that what really is important is their interdependence. Detractions are temporary; their partnership enduring. Both, obviously put their life in the custody of the other. The soldier and his steed—both at attention!

the horse, unencumbered by the rider. If there is any blockage in the flow of energy from the haunches forward, the rider's influence will not help the horse's physical development but rather contributes to his breakdown. The horse can only develop as a total organism, a complete structure. A moving horse' s impact on the ground, with the added burden of the weight of his rider, disturbs the structure and traumatizes the horse's physique, unless the impact of the contact with the ground is correctly absorbed by the horse and distributed throughout his whole body. Elastic musculature and supple, strong joints help to cushion the blows that contact with the ground delivers to the moving horse. Hence, the importance of gymnasticizing to attain these goals is indisputable.

To reestablish the horse's natural balance under the added weight of the rider and tack is the fundamental goal; until this has been attained, one cannot ride the horse safely. However, a further goal must be for the horse to carry himself and the rider with greater efficiency than he would naturally display on a pasture, when relieved of burden. Therefore, we must relentlessly pursue the double, interrelated principles of *straightening the horse in order to ride him forward.* Without ambidextrous efficiency, the hind legs will not *load evenly,* meaning that the horse cannot move either straight or forward correctly. *Moving forward* means that we ask the horse to *amplify his natural gaits* under the rider, and in spite of his weight. We must insist, after having established the horse's natural balance, that he athletically propel *himself and his rider* in amplified gaits. The amplification of the gaits can be either in the direction of extension (greater in or in the direction of collection (greater in height). The horse's "voluntary effort" results in the so-called "ordinary" gaits. They are not only too ordinary to be aesthetically pleasing but are also inefficient. Ordinary gaits may suffice to warm-up or loosen-up the horse before serious demands commence but they are not the crowning achievement of gymnastically developed physiological improvement. The horse's gaits should be eloquent in both their rhythmic demarcation and in their cadence and suspension.

A gymnastically fully developed internationally competing horse should appear to defy gravity. He should tread the ground with graceful ease, rather than fall clumsily onto it.

Some teachers coach their riding clientele in the performance of competition movements only. However, these movements do not have any intrinsic importance other than for evaluating the horse's relaxation, the rhythmic regularity of his gaits, the degree of improved balance and carriage, the degree of increased impulsion and the level of sophisticated engagement of the haunches. Competition movements are not merely gestures, nor are they patterns of choreographic importance.

We must never forget that the rider's commitment is to ride the horse, not to just ride the pattern. Therefore, it would be wiser to create equestrians, for the horse already knows how to be a horse. Beyond the necessary physical skills, which constitute the sport in riding, we need to address the rider's mind, that is, the science of riding, and the rider's spirit. Because horsemanship is based in science, scholastic knowledge is required for the "tools." The "tools" include riding controls or the help of a coach to be properly utilized. Tools in uneducated hands are always dangerous; they are potentially as dangerous to their user as to the subject to which they are applied. Therefore, the education of the rider in the theory of horsemanship is imperative, as is the shaping of the rider' s attitudes, inner emotional climate and character development. A knowledgeable rider with the right attitude will neither trouble nor break down a horse. When done in the right spirit, riding should improve the personality of the rider, causing new virtues to emerge while strengthening old ones.

If we promote riding with an incorrect seat, and incorrect aids, we will only have an accumulation of mistakes. The longer such people ride horses, the more damage they can inflict. Yet correct riding should produce the opposite, for classical horsemanship is *therapeutic riding*. It is aimed at the restorative functions of the horse's natural balance. It is therapeutically concerned with the suppleness of the spine and musculature, and the even-loading efficiencies of the hind legs. Only after having been first restorative and therapeutic can riding also become athletic in its goals and achievements, and thus promote the gymnastic development of the horse's potential. No living creature can be gymnasticized when ill, in pain, uncomfortable, weak, anxious, intimidated or even unhappy. Riding that does not remain at all times attentive to therapeutic and restorative needs of the horse will fail in the attainment of the athletic ones. Only knowledgeable equestrians can address this task.

If we do not pay attention to the development of the rider, we will lose the art. The rider is the proponent of the art of horsemanship, not the horse. As horsemanship is a career and source of livelihood for only a few, its importance for those who ride for pleasure should be even more emphasized. There is a proverb: "Muss ist ein grosser Herr": compulsion is a great master. Today there is less compulsion to become a fine horseman because there is no longer a pragmatic motivation. In the past, when the horse lost its technological utility, it also lost its economic usefulness. Equestrian development is an entirely voluntary activity now, and can only be rooted in a profound love for the horse and an admiration for the traditions of the ancient art of horsemanship.

Demand for riding instruction is steadily increasing, yet
sufficient efforts to develop expert instructors are sadly lacking. The existing vacuum invites less knowledgeable instruction to take the place of expert instruction. Any nation
interested in securing the future of equestrian art will have to
make serious plans to develop their best talent into instructors. I cannot emphasize enough the importance of the education of the rider's mind and attitude. The life of an equestrian involves one's personal inner life and values, and one's
ethics and character traits. There is no question that horsemanship is a science of many branches.

Not unlike the fine arts, horsemanship cannot be learned
only from books; it deals with living creatures and with
dynamic, ever-changing situations. Therefore, the equestrian
arts can be acquired only through long apprenticeship. Learning institutions dedicated to the maintenance of equestrian
traditions, and defying attempts to reinvent horsemanship,
are needed. The arts flourish only in the company of like-
minded individuals, whereas bad horsemanship is *diverse,*
being based on subjective impressions. Only *correct* horsemanship is understood by different individuals, for good
horsemanship verifies itself.

The art of riding is often discussed, especially as being at
serious odds with technically correct horsemanship. However, they do not contradict each other, but rather comple-
ment one another. There can be no "artistic riding" which
does not present a gymnastically, correctly trained horse, for
all of the beauty of the horse depends on his correct movements. There is no artistic value without it being born of
athletic efficiency and the proper gymnastic development. In
horsemanship, only that which is athletically correct can be
aesthetically beautiful; that is the standard of equestrian
beauty. Those who ride like technicians, and try to turn

horsemanship into a new technology, are not producing technically correct horsemanship and remain in opposition to both technically correct and artistically beautiful rides.

Horsemanship is an ancient art. Its body of knowledge is pragmatic and time-tested; it cannot be reinvented. No one can relive the experience of millions of people who rode for millions of hours with millions of thoughts and feelings about it all. Those experiences have been sifted and synthesized for us, into accumulated knowledge that ought to be acquired by aspiring practitioners. All art remains only as good as those who practice it.

Emperors would rather be portrayed enthroned on their horse than on their chair. The horse could portray power, action and elegance. Above all, enthroned on a horse an emperor would be portrayed as greater than by himself. Himself plus virtue. Elevated both literally and symbolically above the pedestrian world.

The skills of horsemanship, the efficient communication of the well-seated, well-aided rider, are the simplest to acquire or teach. Yet we do not pay enough attention to the acquisition of these skills, which provide the most obvious pleasures of riding. These skills are the *sport* in riding.

Competitive riding should be classical riding at its best. Neither the horse nor the human has changed substantially in the last millennium. We could examine analogies from musical performances: riders compete by riding a standard test; pianists play the same composition. Every pianist will sound slightly different, giving a slightly different emotional interpretation or aesthetic emphasis to the same composition. However, the basic skills of being able to play the keyboard efficiently, of practicing, concentrating, focusing, performing, are the same. Only when the basic skills are mastered is energy liberated for artistic interpretation and brilliance. Inartistic performances of tests are performances that lack the basics of correct seat and aids, that lack an understanding of the training goals and represent a careless emotional approach to the art. When all the basics are in place, the now "unselfconscious" rider is liberated to become a "brilliant" performer. Brilliance cannot be planned or contrived because it must be born of perfected technique.

2
Quo Vadis, Dressage?

Should competition challenge or reinforce classical horsemanship?

I want to remind you that dressage riding, classical horse-manship, is an art, and any living art survives by its proponents and exponents. The way we ride is the way it is. Art cannot survive only in books; it cannot exist in notations. Those who go to competitions and display themselves in public are, for most observers, going to represent the art of riding today. It is through the practitioners and petitioners that every art survives or, if not properly practiced, derails and dies.

There were times good horsemanship or ballet disappeared and had to be revitalized, given rebirth. If we let classical horsemanship go wrong for one generation, it will be lost, because it is a living art that survives from mentor to mentor, from teacher to pupil, and is displayed and handed over to a new generation by those who currently represent it. If you permit misrepresentation of a great art derived from two millennia of tradition, we might lose it. If you become its defender, the tradition will be healthy and continue, to the joy and pleasure of all who are professionally dedicated to its survival and progress.

I think what we experience today is very different from what the last four hundred years of classical equitation tradition thrived on. We are witnessing the disappearance of the traditional utilitarian horse. However, the horse has a new and perhaps even more important role than it had in the past, when its primary use was that of a beast of burden and speed. In other words, the horse was technology. Today, the horse's utility is different.

I think we are living in the age of the "super horse" and the minimal rider. We have horses genetically perfected, born beautiful. They are bred and raised so well that there isn't much challenge in making them look supple and rhythmic. These horses move with grandeur, with gorgeously magnified gaits that have length, height, and a liquid, supple, fluent, magnificent motion. They carry themselves voluntarily in a spectacularly beautiful outline. Such horses encourage the arrival of the minimal rider, who has nothing much to do but sit on this magnificent, natural vehicle of beauty and inspiration, and begin to reduce it to the standard of the rider's equitation. They will often convert a magnificently bred gait into a small, choppy, irregular, and eventually uneven stride. They can destroy such a magnificent horse by intimidation, restriction, and confinement and make him unhappy, tense, and an unpleasant sight.

Here is the challenge of our time: how to deal with a generation of riders who, with the help of these magnificent horses, need to understand their obligations and mission. Their coaches and judges should not accept what is simply a technology of manipulating these wonderful creatures to

A century apart in creation yet very similar in message and in posture. Man and horse anchored to the ground but mindful of one another. Each needs not look at the other to know exactly where their partner is in body and mind. A powerful human athlete's strength dwarfed by the horse's. Yet his watchful intellect prevails. Man and horse put shoulder to shoulder, allowing the horse to lead in physical progress but man to give it direction. Their power comes from harmonious understanding of one another. Horse and man in trustful awareness of each other without being blinded to the world around them.

replace equitation. Riders should not be coached in skills that cover up their known training faults and hope that the faults they cannot hide will not be noticed by the judge. Such riders are greedy to ride from victory to victory, even if not to deserved fame, then eventually to notoriety. We must, of course, fight these tendencies and create equestrians who are first and foremost motivated by love for the horse. They should understand and appreciate that they have horses superior to those that upheld this tradition a hundred years ago. Then, riders sat on remounts in the army, green horses who came from casually bred peasant stock and needed years of correct work before they could be supple. Those horses needed to be developed to carry a rider properly, while today we have the luxury and the historically unprecedented joy of being able to purchase horses who come to us with the first two years of work on balance, strength, suppleness, and elasticity seemingly completed for us by superior genetics.

Here is my counsel to you: the horse is a living creature, and when he looks and behaves as if he were a Fourth Level horse ready for the double bridle, don't believe him. He may be young and green, yet beautifully bred and nurtured. He may come to you as a three-year-old, spectacular in a way your ancestors never could have seen. He is not a peasant horse from a village square morning market, yet you still have to develop him, dressage him, as if he were. There can be no shortcuts; there are no tricks and no innovations in classical horsemanship.

A genetically superior new stock of horses is available for the rapidly growing masses interested in horsemanship. This contributes to ignorant horsemanship. When more people want to know something that few experts can teach them, they will inevitably seek out instructors with less than expert qualifications.

Some riders perceive two kinds of qualitative experiences and begin to advocate the existence of two kinds of dressage. They propose that on the one hand, there is a pragmatic, practical way of riding: just going out there, doing the necessary shortcuts, doing the necessary disciplinary action, "muscling" the horse a little, and getting these super horses to super-perform in a super-short time in a super manner because the goal is victory in contests, maybe followed by a quick sale.

I disagree with this point of view, but there are more and more people who have no access to classical equestrian education or lack the will to pursue it, riders who are intellectually lazy, are physically incompetent, and will gladly promote the notion that there is a new kind of dressage akin to technology.

These same people suggest that, on the other hand, there is another kind of dressage which the proponents of the "new dressage" call old fashioned, ivory tower, purist, slow, boring, tedious, nonproductive, and only for the timid. This kind of dressage takes so much time of doing seemingly nothing much of anything significant that one should really not pursue it. This kind of slow and academic dressage belongs to the kind of people who "talk a good ride but never rode one." Yet those who "know" how to "train" understand the usefulness of practical, pragmatic, fast, and even "technologically-aided" new ways of doing things. That, they argue, will inevitably earn you the Blue Ribbon, the only acceptable verification of success and documentation of knowledge according to them.

In my opinion, which agrees with the those principles upheld by the Federation Equestre International (FEI), great successes in competition should reward those who ride the purest, most traditionally acceptable, classical dressage. The FEI organization was created for two purposes: to uphold the classical principles of horsemanship and to insist that only it remains victorious consistently in the competition arena. The FEI, the world equestrian organization that supervises international contests, is also responsible for the development and education of international judges. The FEI was founded to uphold and remains dedicated to the purest principles of classical equitation. They do not subscribe to the view that there are or should be two kinds of dressage. The FEI promotes the notion that only superb riding should remain consistently victorious in the international competition arena.

The proponents of the "new dressage," however, propose that there is training that is faster and more fun than the tedious old ways of "slow and steady." They say there's proof new dressage is better because it is often victorious. There are a lot of riders who win and win consistently who aren't following the slow and steady ways of the classical traditions. How can that be? Easily! There is such a thing as winning by default. You go to shows where you know your fellow contestants are even worse than you are. That is very good insurance for victory. You can go to shows where you know the judge listed hasn't enough understanding or expertise to detect the problems you cover up. So you go, successfully cover up, and win. You can also win because judging is more complex than just monitoring the correct results of classical equitation. It also includes observation of standards of exactitude, precision, and so on, which might contribute points towards success. So, there are indeed some riders whose idea that there is a new dressage which doesn't take a long time to school is sometimes rewarded by victories.

Should we not ask the question, "is competition really the only measure of an equestrian?" No. It never was, it isn't, and it never will be! For ages, for centuries, real horsemanship existed, thrived, and survived without any competition at all. Regimental contests in the military became fashionable about one hundred years ago, but they were few, far between, and very seldom done; those were the beginnings of competition. A rider attended maybe one per year.

One hundred years ago how did people know who were the great riders, the great coaches, teachers, and mentors, the people to imitate? It was an equestrian age and an equestrian society, and people knew who the experts were because the experts are always those respected by their peers. A medical doctor becomes a medical doctor when other doctors say, "I think you can heal and cure." You and I cannot give people a medical degree. Lawyers become lawyers when they pass the Bar Examination and fellow lawyers say, "Yes, this is a solicitor." In those times, the older generation of riding masters said, "Yes, you are one of us." It wasn't an applauding public in the spectators' galleries of an arena; nobody needed to win a Blue Ribbon. Those in the know knew who were the right ones, respected and admired them, and gave them the position to teach and be the mentors of the next generation of riders. This consensus of experts is now missing. It is a very difficult position to be in, because the only vehicle to rank riders' merits has become competition. This is wrong. We must maintain an equestrian community in which there are other guidelines.

I will remind you that the greatest riders are often not competing riders. Many members of the Spanish Riding School don't compete and never did. Others do and win, an encouraging sign that classical horsemanship is still often victorious in the show ring. Remember that great judges, coaches and trainers who are not competing, are often outstanding horseman and superb riders. So are young, not affluent but greatly talented and well schooled riders often absent from competitions. Other riders who pursue the "slow and tedious" ways of classical horsemanship are also victorious. The idea now spreading that successful competition on any level, local or international, should determine the ranking of riders is dangerous and faulty.

I think that when you observe the goals of the FEI, which are stated in Article 401 of the Rule book, on the objects and general principles guiding dressage, you will see that the classical principles are clearly reiterated as the goal for all

Nothing educates quite like a horse. Without losing the meaning by verbalizing abstractions, the horse silently sends his messages. The education prevails. His rider must, and will listen. He will become the better for it. For courage, wisdom born of insight and humility, empathy born of compassion and love, all can be bequeathed by a horse to his rider. The rider becomes the humble recipient of the bounty only his horse can give him. Character improves, virtues multiply, wisdom deepens by the rider's association with his horse.

Yet, there is no chatter. The exchanges are subtle but unmistakable in their meaning. Nothing is lost in understanding when two creatures of nature unite in purpose and remain resolved in their partnership. This interdependence of the strong partner with the smart one forged the character of the leading classes, the elite of Occidental society for centuries. Hence the nobles in most European languages were referred synonymously as riders. For only the nobles were privileged to be allowed to become riders and benefit from the improvements and education only horses could bequeath. Hence one is "knighted" and all knights were on horseback. Chevalier, the rider, is synonymous to the noble. Cavalieri are also. The Ritter is a rider but ennobled. And so it is that in English, French, Italian and German the nobility was called A Rider! No greater title could be born with greater pride.

competition riders: that dressage should be the gradual, rational, scientific development of the horse until he is supple and properly trained to perform. The FEI believes what for generations all good riders believed: that you develop a horse slowly to unfold his natural potential, and incidentally, only incidentally, you can then compete with him on some level suitable to his current development.

No serious riders ever believed the training goal was to compete. They believed that you rode a horse to unfold his natural potential until it was fulfilled and the horse could offer no more physically because he had no more genetically defined talents to display. The goal was not to practice and drill competition movements routinely day after day in order to chisel, hone, and make them routine until the horse performed them like a puppet on a string. That is a reversal of the meaning of horsemanship. Elevating competition to be the end goal of riding, rather than the development of the horse's talent, could derail the tradition of classical equitation.

It should be the other way around. We should ride to do something good for the horse's sake so that he can be beautiful and display himself by his own will to his own advantage. We should not manipulate horses to make them our competition vehicles for winning ribbons. I think it is very important that we raise a generation of riders who understand how competition can be rewarding, but should not become the ultimate goal of horsemanship. We should take much better care of riders' education, reaching not just their bodies but also their minds and attitudes, developing in them interest in the horse's well-being, rather than the superficial interest of winning contests. And I think when a very good rider on a very well-trained horse appears in front of an expert judge, he will inevitably be victorious.

The last, and perhaps biggest, danger is that we live in a technological age. Its guidelines include the principle that things are good if they are new, if they have improved on the old. The old and known ways, by definition, are technologically "passe." In today's computer and sound-reproducing industries, if you wait six months, your equipment is really outdated. You can't even trade it in. We are trained to believe that in a technological age, only innovation succeeds. The new succeeds because it is technologically and mechanically simpler than what it replaces. Anything simple to operate is a success.

We are not here to reinvent classical horsemanship, because everything has been tried, tested, and thought about, and only that which worked most of the time with most horses, in gentle and easy ways, was retained; that is the classical body of equestrian knowledge. It is pragmatic; it is as up-to-date as you can ever get because the horse and the human did not change all that much in two millennia. We don't need a new technology, a new shape and form. We don't need those people who advocate neo-primitivism and want to reinvent things. We have no need for new gimmicks. We have no use for the trick of the month. We have tried everything for centuries, and we are up to date!

The classical rider who takes his time to develop the foundation of the horse, correct musculature, and correct skeletal motion and pursue the purest ideals is the most up-to-date rider in the world. There is no one who can improve on him.

To summarize my assessment of current horsemanship, I find that we are now at a juncture of either going wrong with this wonderful art or preserving the ways we have inherited. The ability to derail classical horsemanship is tempting because we have arrived at the age of the super horse, which superficially represents in the raw some of the features we hope to see years later, due to human induced improvement of the horse.

I trust that the FEI exists to insure that international riding doesn't deteriorate. A second hope is that the horse's new utility is now in sports and that those who love the horse will recognize that a good, beautiful, and fabulous horse deserves as much care by gradual development and knowledgeable nurturing as the "old nag" at the turn of the century. If you recognize that the horse is more worthy of our attention today than he was 400 years ago and we still dedicate ourselves to upholding classical principles, we will allow the best rider on the most correctly developed horse to be victorious in the competition arena.

3
Dressage Needs No Reinventing

The issue at stake is the survival of classical equitation. My thoughts about it are rooted in old convictions about the equestrian tradition and the equestrian art. Writing about these convictions is a result of the needs directly revealed by about a dozen riders with whom we held inspired conversation on this subject. But beyond the inspirational push which I received from these, my favorite equestrians, I have been asked the same or similar questions by dozens of other riders.

The questions prompting this writing include "What is the status of our American dressage? How does it compare to the rest of the world? Are we pursuing the right ideals? Does what we commonly see in competition represent the classical ideals?"

Also, a related set of questions are asked: "Where can I go to learn the right things? Where can I go to even see the right things? Where can I learn all about classical equitation so that I may not only practice it correctly but be able to pass it on to others unaltered, unadulterated, and intact? Is there a program where future instructors are prepared to carry on this living tradition? Where do I turn, where to go, for how long?"

Then again, "How do I get even enough education to distinguish the right instruction or right training from something wrong or compromised? How do I find out? Where are the authorities? Who agrees? What are they agreeing upon?"

Wonderful questions. It is sad that no institution or forum is ready to answer them. How sad it would be if they could learn only from primitive sorcerers or medicine men with Neolithic ideas; if they were seeking, but receiving only half knowledge/half superstition, half soothe saying/half surmising. How sad it would be if the knowledge that now exists and is still available, should disappear for lack of a generation acquiring it. The survival of classical equitation is at stake: there are many who would gladly live, acquire, practice and teach its traditional inheritance, but where can they go to be taught?

Are we ready to accept an "ersatz" dressage, one which is re-invented daily? Are we abandoning the vast wisdom of hundreds of years of accumulated, pragmatic knowledge and mastery without a whimper? Are we giving up on the future schooling of a generation of masters while there are still chances for its education?

"One person with a belief is equal to a force of ninety-nine who have only interests," said John Stuart Mill and there is more than one person left with beliefs and without only interests to pursue.

There are people who wish dressage well and love its truth, which is vested in love and concern for the horse and his proper development. I am convinced that most of my readers share this affection for both the horse and the pursuit of classical equitation. I hope that, born of this affection, the survival of classical equitation will be assured.

"Absence and death are the same—only in death there is no suffering." The absence of beauty and truth in equitation causes pain to those watching misguided horsemanship. For riding is not dead, but classical knowledge is often absent from it. Poor riding, incorrect training, and unhappy horses are often not caused by wrong intentions but rather by the unavailability of the right guidance. We urgently need to educate those who are fit to pass on this noble tradition to assure the future of correct equestrian growth.

There is an encouraging loudness to the chorus of those seeking the right knowledge. They should make real demands on the equestrian community to supply them with institutions where the right knowledge can be learned through the right means!

It is not enough to have a suspicion that the right knowledge does exist; more and more riders reading good dressage books, looking analytically at photographs or reproductions of old pictures and engravings, are recognizing that horses and riders might look and behave differently from those they sometimes observe.

Fortunately we have access to internationally accepted and admired authorities, who talk about the correct goals in judges' forums and various seminars and clinics. Listening to them, one not only is privileged to hear the classical principles of horsemanship re-stated and the essentials of it re-emphasized, but one realizes that dressage cannot be re-invented! Indeed, it should not be re-invented, for its traditions are valid and should be scrupulously adhered to.

Dressage can be learned, by taking a long time and making an honest effort, but it cannot be replaced by inventions. For in this art newness does not represent improvement as in a detergent; rather, age-old wisdom is the only assurance of superior quality in training. Those who act like neo-primitives, ignoring the entire massive body of knowledge, wisdom, and practice handed to us for centuries, will seasonally re-invent horsemanship as their fumbles blossom into seasonal technologies.

No one entering medical school expects fumbling to be a part of instruction. They rather expect to be given a condensed approximation of all the medical wisdom to date. They have the intention of honoring this knowledge, assimilating it as best they can, and hope for the future chance to add to this their most considered wisdom, by new discoveries or inventions. This is the accepted procedure in all human endeavor based on knowledge. Take something as simple as asking for a light: one does not expect someone to re-invent fire by rubbing sticks together, but rather one hopes for a lighter.

It should be considered one's privilege to learn the grandeur of the past, the well-tested, time-honored principles of the past riding masters. There should be places to go to learn about these! I hope that the many educational dressage organizations will soon see it as their major mission to assure for the future the proper education of a continuous body of dressage instructors.

As in all arts, the equestrian art must be based on apprenticeship. It cannot be assimilated by "shopping around" for ideas and inspirations. Even a discriminating mind, a discerning perception, depends on properly grounded knowledge; ignorance causes gullibility. However, combining good information with insight one can seek out knowledgeable tutoring.

Then comes a revelation, finally feeling that a horse behaves gymnastically correctly, and the new convert displays a fervor the likeness of which has not been known since the

The commanding of armies was done from horse back. Life and death depended on the visibility and credibility of commanding authority. His horse in passage, confident, attentive, obedient, lends his rider the leisure to look over his followers. He needs no stirrups for safety but beyond that riding without stirrups was regarded as a gesture of humility towards both the horse and the art of riding him.

conversion of Paul of Tarsus on the road to Damascus. St. Paul died a martyr, while our rider has an alternative to martyrdom, for he has youth, time, and energy left to recover the vast knowledge which eluded him in the past.

Serious aspirants in the arts accepted with joy the humility, tedium, and discipline of apprenticeship. Michelangelo, as a boy, did not think of re-inventing sculpture. Rather he was apprenticed to the master, Pollaiuolo, in order to learn the vast heritage of the past. While doing so, he lived with his master, breathed his atmosphere, and benefited from the informal portions of his education as much as the hours he spent in formal training. While the arts are a product of the mind and the emotions, they are nevertheless still bound to wisdom, and bonded to stubborn laboring.

The arts are not based on skills alone. The skill of equestrian art, to be sure, is the sport of riding. But acquisition of that skill will not make an equestrian! Skills are an important part, but only a part of horsemanship.

None of the great artists in any field, be it painting, dancing, music or architecture, have re-invented their art! None went arrogantly to seek out only technique and technology from their masters. None allotted to their masters only a week-end or ten days into which to compress superficially the techniques that can appear as knowledge to superficial onlookers. Instead, great masters learned all that the past offered and went on to build on it and perhaps to humbly add to it. Their contribution was civilized, because it was in the context of an artistic tradition, rather than a barbaric reinvention of that which already had its own history.

Apprenticeship may be unattractive. It takes much time and effort; it reeks of subservience. As with anything that needs discipline, as horsemanship does, and as with anything that has to do with exacting learning as riding does, the terrible burden of acknowledging ignorance is asked of the pupil. In an age of instant fixing, superficial expertise, and misinterpreted egalitarianism, the horror of having to accept a master who knows more, who must demand, who will supervise, and who has the right to punish, is virtually unacceptable to the arrogant and the presumptuous. But it is precisely these people who should be discouraged and weeded out by the apprentice system, leaving the available space for those who are truly dedicated and willing to sacrifice, those who have the predisposition and the personality to carry on the equestrian tradition.

Equestrian knowledge is not transferable only through books. One rides not by recipes, but by coaching and monitoring. The nature of the art makes it more dependent on apprenticeship than nearly any other, except perhaps dancing.

"If you wish to reach the highest, begin at the lowest." This ancient principle is the most important one for an equestrian to remember. Apprenticeship requires the humility to begin as the lowest.

We make our lives significant, even on this minor planet which is part of an unimportant solar system in an insignificant galaxy, by asking questions about who we are, what our purpose is, and how to do well. The answers become significant only in the light of another's love and acknowledgment. Whether this other is a human or a horse, the justification of our existence will come from being valued by another. "Make yourself necessary to somebody," said Emerson and I would add, then cherish the one to whom you have become necessary!

4
Equestrian Culture and the Whole Person

Apprenticeship is indispensable for the acquisition of equestrian craftsmanship. The discipline of riding presents such a variety of circumstances, due to the variety of individual horses, that only through daily guidance and diversification can the sport be successfully pursued.

More importantly, instruction in equestrian academies should address the entire person, and thus develop the equestrian as a personality. For the sport of riding and the equestrian skills themselves will suffer if the teacher's personality is not properly developed, if his knowledge is not exhaustive and his commitment to uphold the proper principles lacks courage.

I wish to discuss some ideals of great relevance to equestrian development, the kinds of "important intangibles" on which the equestrian understandings are based. These are selected examples among innumerable ones, all which have a place in an academic apprenticeship program.

The Ancient Greeks, who through Xenophon fathered

classical horsemanship, believed that beauty is expressed by harmony which is born of perfect balance. While ample evidence of this maxim may be seen in architectural remains and sculptural fragments from those times, these principles can also be applied to human nature, as they were by the Greeks themselves.

The Ancient Greeks believed the body, mind, and soul to be the three components of a person. These three facets of a rider must always be in perfect balance. The cultivation of one at the expense of the other two components will result in disharmony and discord. However, when equally cultivated and attended to, they will produce a harmonious partnership, which expresses itself in beauty.

These Greek aesthetic ideals were so meaningful that all Occidental art remains but a continuous footnote to them. An equestrian, therefore, ought to develop all three of his personal dimensions, not emphasizing only the body through the sport of riding, but the mind and soul as well.

In equestrian terms, these ideals about the harmonious interaction of the body, mind, and soul become highly significant. The concept of the "soul" need not have a religious connotation even though it could, but might stand for the emotional dimension of one's personality, as opposed to the logical, rational and the physical.

For the horse and rider to appear as merged in the effort of motion such as with the image of the Centaur, "the smart partner on the legs of the strong partner." The rider must offer his mind to guide the body of the horse, while both of their spirits are animated by the joy of this partnership.

So it transpires that beauty is born of the well-honed mind of a human guiding the strong limbs of his mount into a powerful stride, performed in graceful carriage, while both exalt in a partnership born of spirited love, a love which is only heightened by understanding through discipline.

For centuries, horses were a means to educate the elite in all societies where the horse was known. They were man's partners, enhancing his status not only by their imposing sight, but by conveying to the beholder that in the saddle an equestrian, in all his virtue, was enthroned.

For it was only through the training of a horse, through riding one, that the virtues of a man could emerge. In ages past, it was believed that character develops by first hand experience and cannot be formed by secondary, theoretical learning. That virtue emerges through the consistent practice of virtue itself. That human character is not an abstraction but a reality revealed by its daily manifestations. In short, one could not talk a good equestrian line.

The horse could and did give a man a total education. He had to be tamed and befriended, and could not be fooled by honeyed words. Thus, only those who had the humility to blame failures on themselves and never on their mount could benefit from the education a horse could offer. All others, those who blame their failure on their horses and deny their own role as the "smart partner," can never experience character growth.

The humble, however, who look for the remedy to their mistakes in themselves, will recognize their own imperfections, will seek corrections, and will ultimately experience the growth of virtue.

Ennobling character changes will follow. The rider's attention span will lengthen, endurance and the tolerance of pain and discomfort will increase. They will be braver, stronger in body, mind and spirit. Their powers of concentration will deepen to a meditative state, oblivious of anything outside the harmonious absorption of their communion with the horse. Their focus will sharpen to cut the irrelevant details away, making them steadfast in body, mind and spirit. Wiser in analysis, more resourceful in synthesis, they find their task and do it with dispatch. Profound empathy, born of love for the horse, tempered by respect, urged on by a growing tolerance, they become masters of the horse with enough humility not to displease him!

Reluctant to punish, finding it both distasteful and less effective than rewarding, even when in anger, their friendship and bond with their horse never ceases to deepen. Rewarding, even when angry, the supreme courtesy to a respected friend, is frequent, even continuous!

And so the equestrian is formed by practice, the man of virtue emerges by habits internalized, the character becomes ennobled, not by birth but by insight into and perfection of the equestrian arts.

The great craftsmanship, the technology of riding, is based on an aiding system bequeathed to us through the ages by riding masters. This system includes only the most pragmatic, the most utilitarian knowledge; things that on the whole, in the majority of cases, will work! The tradition of aiding is based on the philosophy that horses will perform when *helped* rather than *compelled*, that only a happy frame of mind will result in a relaxed frame for the body, and that compulsion soils the mind and spoils the body with tensions.

The meaning of any aiding, not just as regards to horses, presumes a recognition of a need which one proposes to fill pleasantly. Thus when flood victims are aided, the result is relief, not increased suffering. Similarly, when a horse is aided, we should be able to presume that the rider administers to the horse's needs pleasantly, and that improvement ought to follow.

Indeed the strong partner challenges the smart partner in the equine-human relationship. All equestrians know that by backing a horse their control increases. A man on the ground must know how to prevail yet without losing a spirited friend. To equestrians it is an obvious and often experienced scene beautifully sculpted. Yet, ultimately, it is a monument to the partnership of man and his horse because they both devote their full attention to the other. Even the palatial surroundings can do no more than serve as a backdrop to the important connection between horse and rider which makes them both oblivious to the magnificence of their surroundings.

In direct contrast to aiding is the application of force or compulsion which will cause unpleasant fears and tensions, creating unhappiness. No lover of horses enjoys that reaction from his partner. The more correctly one aids, the better the horse will feel, resulting in becoming increasingly receptive to aiding, and more educable by the process. For aiding is a perpetual, subtle form of rewarding! Thus, the horse becomes more educable as education proceeds correctly. No creature fails to recognize aid, when it is offered to assist him in doing something better and in doing it with less effort.

In human terms, a successful invention is anything that increases leisure and rest and decreases work. The universal catering to laziness and pleasure, the saving of muscular effort, the improvement of efficiency are all winning inventions. All creatures, humans and horses included, will appreciate any absence of pain and will love any entrance of pleasure.

Aids, being gestures of help, build confidence and induce

Whether seated on a horse two thousand years ago, or walking by him in our century, men are depicted in the nude. The horse bares all about his rider. Leaving nothing to imagination, the rider appears in the spiritual nudity of utter frankness, stripped of his pretentious draping. The reciprocity of power and energy ennobles both creatures beyond the character they project by themselves. The configuration of these vastly different creatures as a pair, far surpasses the potential of their composite parts. They are more beautiful together than they could ever be separately.

resultant submission of the horse to the rider's will. This submission is born of trust and verified by harmony, while the use of force might create a servitude born of fear of punishment. Use of force creates apprehension which leads to unpredictable acts of desperation by the horse. We call that, for lack of humility, disobedience; such acts are born of fear, not of calculation. They are human-induced, not horse-conspiratorial!

Aiding always leads to the development of a relaxed horse, enjoying his work, while compulsion leads to a sullen tense and disobedient behavior.

Beauty ultimately looks like the manifestation of happiness. Much more scarce than beauty is the ability to recognize it and allow oneself to be captivated by it.

A frequently ignored element in the pursuit of all passions, including the passion for the equestrian arts, is romance. We tend to become passionately involved only when the ambiance appeals to our own romantic sense. Thus the attendant atmosphere to riding is, in my belief, not peripheral, but on the contrary, central to its passionate pursuit. The accessories belonging to the equestrian atmosphere, the beauty of a saddle, the feel of a glove, the elegance of boots, the glamour of an heirloom stock pin, all create enormous appeal, none less than the attentive eyes of our horse or his ears, his soft submission to the harmony of our aiding system.

Most important to equestrian ambiance and the fostering of the proper atmosphere is the behavior of its practitioners. This presumes that equestrians, wherever they appear, ought to recognize one another just by observing behavioral patterns. The proper posture in standing and sitting; the quieting of speech and slowing of motion in the presence of horses; the stroking of the horse, rather than the tapping of his skull when wanting to please him. Conversely, any equestrian atmosphere will be shattered by shrieking and hollering the length of a stable to greet a friend; by egocentric attention-getting giddiness, the permanently fostered empty loud cheerfulness of a barn clientele. Neither feeling the need of the horse nor caring to submit to it, they come around "to have a ball" but not to take their position in life at the horse's side.

To be an equestrian is to take a stance in life. It is a position in life; not to be born into, but cultivated, acquired. We need to develop schools that will foster that stance. Schools that will insure that equestrian education is the by-product of the correct understanding in the mind, and a correct attitude in the spirit. The equestrian stance is all-inclusive of life, for it is an internalized philosophy manifesting itself in daily actions, not just when in the saddle. Without acquiring this knowledge and understanding its meaning, no future generation of equestrian greats can emerge.

The age of the utilitarian horse is over. But the horse as an object of art, as a subject of concern, as a monument to character development is now more important than ever. That which is irreplaceable and not interchangeable deserves cherishing.

5
The Road to Dressage

All good riding is "dressage riding" if we accept the time-honored principle that dressage riding represents classical equitation. Dressage does not exist alone in a vacuum; classical horsemanship includes many phases of horsemanship and a diversity of competition goals. Dressage riding comprises many skills, several of which are acquired by jumping and riding cross-country, or on trails.

There cannot be competitive, specialized dressage riding without first simply becoming a good rider. A good rider is, by definition, a diversified equestrian athlete who is willing and able to generalize any horse's training before specializing strictly in "dressage" (gymnastics) schooling for purposes of competition. Dressage work serves many ends; dressage, the taming and training of any horse according to classical principles, certainly remains the fundamental means for various specialized goals.

However, the converse is also true. No one can specialize a horse for dressage competitions until he has first used alternate means for the strengthening of the horse's body and the improvement of his character. An educated horse is not

Even the winds blow from all directions, contributing to the curvilinear turbulence of this baroque monument. Classical horsemanship as we pursue it today is still a baroque art, much like grand opera. The images of beautiful horsemanship contain the important elements of the Baroque aesthetic style. The Baroque understanding of the world is that nature is grand but not perfect until human intelligence interferes in its behalf. Perfecting the potential of nature is the challenge of human intelligence and wisdom. To understand how to improve on nature's random beauty by human design, is, indeed, the baroque understanding of what aesthetics are. The taming, honing, trimming of horrendous nature into something predictable by design is the task. Yet one must understand the essential nature of what one undertakes to improve. Fulfillment of natural potential comes by knowing the nature of the potential. Artifice, disrespect for the essential nature of things in this world, would violate the Baroque quest for ideals.

The last valuable guidance in the equestrian arts came from the 18th century, from the times of the height of the Baroque civilization.

However, the style also included a taste for opulence and grandeur. The times of the absolutist monarchs reigning over European populations lead into Baroque taste for excesses, especially in decoration and beauty. Therefore, horsemanship as we cultivate it in its ideal form of inherited wisdom, includes not merely the Baroque guiding philosophies but its taste for emotionally unsurpassable evocation of decorative opulence. Without the horse, the style could not have happened.

For what, if not a horse, can become grand, turbulent, romantic and excessive, even while under the tutoring, honing and edification of his nature by human intellect and insight?

merely a specialist. In fact, specialized performance horses reach their highest potentials only because their specialization was well founded by diversification. The basics, for physical development as well as character development, can only be born of diversification.

Any rider who is "doing dressage" in order to avoid cross-country work, cavaletti and jumping because these activities frighten him, is certainly a rider of great contradictions. Overcoming one's fear of falling and fear of the horse and his motion is essential; without this, horsemanship should not be pursued and cannot succeed. No one can fancy himself as schooling a horse in the art of dressage unless he has the equitation skills that make for safety through balance, fitness, excellent health and the wisdom to know the nature of his horse.

Surveying the background and education of great dressage trainers and competitors today, as well as the best of the recent past, you will find that they emerged from diversified, athletically well founded backgrounds. I know that many of the greatest German, Swedish, Danish, Hungarian and British dressage riders, emerged from combined training or eventing backgrounds. Such riders tend to agree that their outstanding dressage performances and training on the highest levels would not have succeeded without their indispensable eventing background. That is why the combined events are nicknamed the "king of the equestrian sports," for one who performs all three phases of riding successfully can later choose specialization and succeed again.

I have written and lectured often on the subject of the compatibility and coexistence of dressage and jumping, both in the interest of the horse and of the rider. Dressage and jumping (combined training) are complementary rather than mutually exclusive. Unquestionably, the development of all-around equine and human athletes depends on practice over varied terrain, jumps, and a formal school for gymnasticizing on the level ground.

The "Campaign school" of equitation is based on the belief that horses develop all of their foundation work outside on the "open countryside" (French *campagne*). Only later are horses ready, as a consequence of improved strength and balance, to benefit from work in the confinement and artificiality of a proper dressage school (manege), with its frequent successions of rounding sharp corners to move on to short but straight lines. The more difficult figures of the manege require, of course, even greater athletic sophistication from the horse and his guiding influence, the rider. Horses too weak, clumsy or unbalanced to move safely and efficiently over natural terrain will certainly not be shining stars in the manege when dressage performance is called for.

Terribly harmful for the cause of good equestrian education is the mistaken belief that dressage will ruin good jumpers. Knowledgeable riders who also possess a sound theoretical education know that dressage helps jumpers. For good jumping is always the result of how the horse is brought to the fence and how he departs from it. Balance, rhythm, regularity, engagement, attention, the ability to shift the center of gravity quickly, etc. are the fundamental necessities for jumping success. They are also the alpha and omega of dressage! Unfortunately, some jumping riders might see "false dressage" and be disgusted by it. So are, of course, educated dressage riders. A horse in "false collection" with mincing, shuffling, irregular strides with the grim nature of a docile slave surely cannot inspire the imagination of a jumping rider.

Let us not forget that a well-stretched and correctly formed, developed and maintained "topline" is essential to both suc-

More than two thousand years ago the Greeks understood the deep, adhesive, independent seat. Unity of horse and rider impeccably maintained even in the turbulence of battle. Horses were anchored on their haunches in moments of their greatest exuberance. The agility of horsemanship is born of harmonious unity between horse and rider. Here animation is made beautiful.

cessful dressage and jumping riding. The "bascule" is the longitudinal flexion prerequisite for dressage riders in order to perform their best.

International competitive participation and good coaching as well as the best of the equestrian literature bear witness that dressage helps jumping and jumping helps dressage. The experts believe that specialization succeeds only after generalization and diversification. This ideology is relevant to both horses and riders.

A dressage instructor who knows nothing about cross-country, cavaletti or jumping is not necessarily a good choice for a serious pupil. Lack of expertise in horsemanship is certainly not confidence-inspiring. Nor should riders prematurely fancy themselves as beyond the need for riding diversity and the pursuit of cross-country, cavaletti and trail work. If they do, they often will arrive at incorrect equitation and compromised gymnastic results.

There can be no denial that *courage* is the prime equestrian virtue, indeed it is the prime virtue of life. Without it, none of the other virtues can develop. So it is essential for riders to involve themselves in activities that demand courage greater than the manipulation of a docile horse in a fenced-in school. Horses are powerful, regardless of wishful thinking or limited experience that might make riders believe otherwise. Without courage, a horse cannot be educated by any rider and therefore will remain, or become all the more dangerous. Disobedient and unpredictable is the sour, hassled, bored, confined horse!

A good coach increases the courage of the rider and the horse. This confidence is born of improvement of skills, familiarity with diverse tasks and the knowledge of the horse's nature under varying circumstances. Specialized and limited experience increase the danger inherent in horsemanship. They also deny the opportunity to fully develop both the horse and rider's inherent potential for athletic performance as a unit.

6
Reasons for
Academic Equitation

The horse, by nature, is an animal who should not, and cannot, carry you easily. He is not an animal of burden by any means.

Examination of the horse's musculature and skeleton reveal that he is not an animal that should have anything on his back at all if we want to keep him healthy, happy, and moving beautifully. He is better suited to pulling since his motor force derives solely from the hindquarters. Therefore, he is most suited for running.

The majority of the horse's weight happens to be in front of, and not on top of the hindquarters. As a consequence the forehand serves as a crutch to support this weight. Humans, whose legs support all their weight *and* provide locomotion, move easily and gracefully. Pushing a heavy wheelbarrow or a hand plow will simulate the horse's problem: pushing a majority of his weight from behind. So the horse's natural tendency is to put his weight on the forehand and push it by a kicking motion against the ground, catapulting forward with as much speed as possible; thus the Thoroughbred on the racetrack most approximates the activity for which the horse was really made—to take flight.

When you hitch a carriage or buggy behind the horse, he is not unhappy because his weak points are not taxed by a burden on top of him and he can thrust his weight forward to pull this light and reasonably mobile item. The source of locomotion is then in the center of the entire moving unit, making the horse's task easy. But a horse is not designed to carry additional weight on his back. And yet we make him do this.

We not only expect him to live happily ever after, but optimistically expect him not to break down. We also expect him to move well, even better than nature would inspire him to move. This is a tremendous task that we assign to ourselves and the horse. We must set about it properly, because if we make a mistake anywhere, we damage the musculature and the joints of the horse faster than we can feel sorry about it.

If you look at a horse's haunches, his power source, you see four joints: hip, stifle, hock and fetlock. In order for the horse to propel himself forward with the weight of the rider and equipment without damaging these joints, we must gymnastically develop the animal gradually and systematically.

The idea is similar to the development of a human gymnast. What does a gymnast do to look so fabulously coordinated and so beautiful in action? A gymnast has developed his joints and musculature properly, so that with minimum effort, strain and caloric output, he can perform movements of incredible power with maximum grace.

Similarly, the goal of equine gymnastics, dressage, is to develop the kind of gymnast who with minimum effort floats in suspension above the ground with utmost grace and coor-

Dignity, gravity, authority, all because of his horse's expression, his undivided attention. This privilege and being enthroned in the saddle animated many would-be rulers and dictators to make processions and grand entrances on horseback. Nothing seems more reassuring to both the would-be leader and the populace in need of leadership than to see one offered on horseback.

dination. This is the goal that we propose to pursue.

In order to develop muscular strength and elasticity and supple joints, we must put the horse through very careful and progressive gymnastic exercises. However, if the exercises are not careful and progressive, they will break down part or all of the horse's locomotive system. You know very well that if you overburden a horse following incomplete training, he will likely tie up, or worse yet, develop azoturia, which can cause death.

In the human realm, look at a laborer. In the course of a day, he will work at least as hard as, if not more than, most athletes do in the course of heavy training. Yet he seldom possesses the full, finely sculpted body of the gymnast, nor will he move with the gymnast's elegance, and will often appear broken down, even emaciated. Because he did not develop and does not use his body properly, he cannot have that coordinated grace. But a trained gymnast who works out eight hours daily will look beautiful. His musculature will develop in the right places, and he will coordinate and move with graceful form and brilliance. Both the laborer and the gymnast work the same number of hours and sweat equally heavily, yet one becomes a beautiful human being while the other can become a broken down person.

As a rider, and therefore the trainer of your horse, you will determine which direction your horse's development will take. To say, "I'm working my horse, and he will be great," is not necessarily so. If you work a horse the wrong way, you will ruin him. You will make him a prematurely aged, stiff, broken-down, unhappy creature full of pain.

When you look at the joints of the hindquarters, it is important to understand that the hock is a smaller joint than the human knee. The human knee carries only one hundred to two hundred pounds, yet it is commonly the site of arthritis, pain, swelling; it is predisposed to injury. And the horse's hock carries from one thousand to fifteen hundred pounds. In the trot and canter, gaits with moments of suspension, the force absorbed by the joints is even greater than fifteen hundred pounds. Added to the gravitational force is the kinetic energy of descent and the considerable force exerted by the horse in his propulsive thrust.

And if that hock absorbs impact in the wrong way and is not allowed to carry the burden with an elastic flexion, we will make that hock defend itself against the resultant pain and injury. That hock joint will build up scar tissue and cartilage which will be very painful.

This is why you see so many horses with a "hitching hock." These horses are unlevel, meaning one hind leg moves shorter than the other, an impure movement. The horse is not clinically lame, nor would a competition judge eliminate him. This kind of problem is called "rein lameness" because it is introduced by the rider using his hands rudely or ignorantly. If you sustain pressure on the horse's jaw for a long time or pull on the horse's mouth hard and consequently contract his neck, he will have to oppose that pressure because nature gave him a certain length of neck musculature that needs to be carried in a comfortable stretch in order to be relaxed and without pain.

If the rider, for any reason, tries to compact the horse's neck, it hurts the horse, just as tight shoes hurt one's toes. Soon the horse will likely pit his very strong neck musculature against the rider's hand power and pull on the bit even after he has already made his jaw stiff by opening it in an attempt to release the offending pressure. Since the awful hand comes back with the gaping jaw and insists on further torturing, the horse has no alternative but to pit his strong neck musculature against the pulling arm. It takes two to pull!

The horse stiffens and pulls in an effort to save his hocks from the whiplash that results from the tug of war in front. It is hurting him! So if you participate in this pulling contest, the horse comes down so hard on his joints and kicks the ground with so much defiant force as he fights the torturous pain in his mouth and neck that he eventually breaks down either one or both hocks, depending on single or two-handed pulling by the rider.

The other extreme results from work on the so-called "light hacking rein." You can be equally rude with a dropped rein, because when somebody asks you to come to the middle of the ring or to the walk from the trot, you take the up the now loose rein suddenly and it gives an inevitably strong yank and rip at the jaw. At that moment the horse becomes alarmed and whiplashes back to the hock, a painful jolt against which nature builds up arthritic tissues.

So whether it is a perpetually pulling hand or an occasionally rough, abrupt hand, you must know that every time you use your hands improperly, you are assuring your horse shortened usefulness and an unhappy life.

Why do so many riders not leave the horse's mouth alone? One possible reason for this fault is that we are a visually and manually oriented society. We always want to see what we are doing. And the only area of the horse that one sees is his neck and head. And one is so mesmerized by the beauty, agility and power of that neck that one wants to get involved, shape it, dominate it, intimidate it. This is one reason riders "move into" the horse's head and take up residence there. Heavy handedness also results from the "too much, too soon" method. Before the rider has an independent, relaxed and balanced seat, he is allowed to handle the reins.

Traditionally, riders were lunged, sometimes up to eighteen months, until a perfectly independent balanced seat emerged. Only then was the rider allowed to control the horse's mouth and contact the reins. He who lacks a secure seat will find himself in an extremely vicious circle of losing balance and being frightened of falling, grabbing for the reins as one who seeks a handle to grasp for balance. We don't try to regain our balance with our toes or our ear lobes; it's always our hands.

It would be best if riders understood how to begin to learn to ride and invested the time to learn to sit properly in the correct balance and the correct relaxation so that their hands become independent of their seats. Then they could use them independently, rather than dependently, to steady themselves.

Riding is a sport of slow development. Yet it is rewarding because one can pursue it into old age and ride in some cases into one's eighties. Correct development of riding skills is slow, complex and disciplined work. Only the acquisition of the proper skills ensures riding pleasure.

7
Classical Horsemanship Makes a Harmonious Partnership

Many branches of horsemanship exist because there were, historically, many uses for the horse. Classical horsemanship, however, has emerged as the only type of horsemanship that pursues goals *respectful of* the horse's needs. Other riders use the horse for transportation, work and running after a polo ball, only goals desired by the rider. Classical horsemanship is dedicated to the promotion of the horse's well-being: longevity, soundness and a good life. To promote these ideas we must develop the horse's athletic potential to its fullest extent.

All horses instinctively desire a pain free life and dedicated horsemen join their horse in its pursuit. Success can be measured by the rider's ability to promote the horse's painlessness and even his sense of pleasure while the horse carries his rider. Therefore, in this partnership, the horse and the rider both are concerned with the horse's well-being. This is the most valid foundation for a successful team.

Classical horsemanship's goal orientation is first restorative, then therapeutic, and then gymnastic. The tradition of kindness to horses was based on pragmatic goals. Men, if lacking higher motivation, even out of selfishness, had to share the horse's ambition for a painless existence. Without it, horses could have not lived a long serviceable life.

Horses were valuable and therefore a symbol of power; their riding and training, indeed, was a privilege. Horses were the most important "technology" at man's disposal: they could multiply man's muscular strength and increase his speed of travel. The very definition of any technology includes the properties of saving human energy and conserving the consumption of time for a task.

In contemporary technological societies, however, the horse's pragmatic value has sharply diminished. As technology increased, his usefulness became incidental and he emerged as a luxury item with value relating to recreation and pleasure. As such, people can regard horses as dispensable and their value for pleasure may include flaunting vanity and displaying power.

Thus, for the first time in history, we may volunteer but do not have to remain loyal to the well-being of the horse. We can live without a horse and those who can afford to ride them may well be able to afford to replace them.

Fortunately, man's age-old reward for correct horsemanship was its pleasure. When correctly pursuing horsemanship, the rider works in harmony with his horse. He can believe that the horse reads his thoughts and senses his wishes. Harmony born of the bodily skills of good equitation and of right-mindedness will allow the horse to instantly and uncompromisingly oblige our wishes. This obligation may give us the illusion that our thought has replaced the will of the horse and that our wishes are unconditionally carried out by the horse.

The delight of the great equestrian, however, is the horse's willing submission to his wishes. Born of confidence that the decisions are for pleasure, the horse seeks his rider's guidance. He submits in recognition that our intentions are identical with his needs.

A horse's submission should never be that of a slave. Even tyrants lack interest in the submission of the weak and always seek to intimidate and control the strong and courageous. Nor is there any pleasure in riding a horse that behaves like a mechanized puppet. Only a horse with a good mind, a powerful personality, pride, courage and grandeur in motion is an intriguing subject for submission. However, we want his submission to be voluntary; we must earn it, not impose it. Only that accomplishment will honor us. When the horse submits his attention to our disposal, he surrenders the energies of his haunches to our use and offers his back to carry us. He serves, but with pride, and the recognition that we honor that service. Respect between horse and rider must be mutual; in that sense, we surrender to him too.

Harmony between horse and rider cannot develop without impeccable equitation. Nothing is more uncomfortable for the horse than a rider out of balance, tense and tight, influencing him without any sense of rhythm. A rider should never appear to a horse as an invader of his privacy. Instead, he should seem part and parcel to his physiognomy, participating within his motion and of the same mind.

A great thrill, resultant of correct equitation, is a sense of weightlessness in motion. An age old desire to soar weightless, to fly faster than our center of gravity allows, to glide, all are granted by the horse that is sat upon correctly. The effortless merger of our center of gravity with that of our horse's can provide the sensation of flight unencumbered by speed and weight. This physical thrill is the reward for great riders.

But intellectual and emotional satisfaction exists as well. There is an endless scholastic challenge to how horses can develop their natural resources, how they can fulfill their potential. There is also an unending emotional challenge of how to control and improve our character in order to better serve the horse.

We sometimes see but must not emulate riders motivated

Only the beauty of efficiency in function could be added to the great natural beauty born by the horse. Nature gave birth to such power and swiftness and gave the sensitivity to quickness of mind through alertness. Man with a purpose can amplify nature given grace. And so it is that we continue to survive together.

by incorrect goals because they may lack love and respect for the horse. These riders seem to have no appreciation for the emotional implications and do not take into account the character developing aspects of horsemanship. They do not pursue horsemanship scholastically, scientifically or intellectually. They perceive riding merely as a sport and take pleasure only in its being a highly competitive one. For these riders, riding becomes competition-dependent for its rewards.

Performance should mean something is worthy of evaluation. That evaluation is based on knowledgeable standards. Should there be nothing worth evaluating nor the expertise to evaluate with, competition would merely be an act, an appearance, an event. To a knowledgeable judge, a performance in the show ring is only acceptable in terms of the standards and traditions of classical horsemanship. The greater the harmony between horse and rider during a performance, the higher rating it merits from an expert judge.

When one is called to evaluate equestrian talent, not performance, which is a result of talent combined with educated skills, one looks for these abilities:

1. To maintain the center of gravity of the rider with that of the horse's and an equal facility to distance that center of gravity from the horse's for purposes of aiding to produce favorable change.

2. To monitor and maintain the horse's rhythmic regularity. The rider must sense every horse's entirely individual conformation, and dependent, rhythmic system. He must harmonize with each horse's innate rhythmic "signature" and know it as individually as knowing fingerprints. By participating initially within the horse's signature rhythm, a rider can induce favorable changes.

3. To monitor the energy level of the motion of the horse and regulate it according to need. To sense a lack of energy or restlessness and be able to change into impulsion for the most efficient carriage and the most harmonious balance at the moment. Such riding abilities foster a successful team.

A judge realizes that in each class there will certainly be one person who will appreciate one's judgment and fully approve of its results: the winner. Others might have reservations. Aware of statistics one knows the odds against winning are approximately 24:1. Therefore, no one should ride in competition who is embittered by not winning each class entered. Surely there are other valid measuring sticks for good horsemanship.

Certainly in the rider's terms, horsemanship can be measured according to the relative improvement of the horse with the passage of time. Regardless of how the horse places in competitions, every rider senses any progress or deterioration developing. If a horse is progressing well due to competition, that then is a success. However, to win in competition with a bad ride is not a sign of success.

We all are reasonable evaluators of our own performance. We can also evaluate the expertise of the judge. A good judge's scores and commentary will correspond with what a knowledgeable rider feels during performance.

We should never aim to learn to ride only for the sake of guiding a horse through a competition test with certain efficiency. We should not seek to build riding skills that attempt to cover up incorrect training results. Instead, we should learn to ride so that our honest performance becomes a by-product of impeccable training procedures. Let awareness of who admires our efforts and who shuns it be the guide of success; let the harmony with our horse verify it.

8
Non-Confrontational Horsemanship

Dressage is the scholarly, systematic and gradual development of the horse's natural potentials, through means which are academically observant of the horse's nature and are guided by love and kindness towards the horse.

Therefore, only those training means are acceptable which are non-confrontational. To force a horse to do anything is in violation of the scholastic observation of his nature and void of guidance motivated by love and kindness. One may ask the horse to do things. One must teach him both the understanding of the communication means (aids) and the ways in which he should deliver his correct performance (showing athletic progress). Knowledgeable riding, indeed, is recognizable by a conspicuous absence of compulsion and confrontation. No force should be applied to gain phony obedience. Rather, time must be spent on the gradual development of the horse's understanding of both the communications and his performance skills and athletic prowess. The aids, the 'language of riding,' can be patiently taught to a horse only by repeatedly explaining the correct responses we expect . Any understanding of communications should be rewarded to reinforce the delivery of correct responses. Undesirable behavior or misreading the signals should be 'punished' by the mildest available means, certainly without causing pain! Such mild forms of punishment may include simply an omission of reward or the application of aids to repeat the command for the same performance desired.

The non-confrontational training principles occur in four conceptual categories:

1. Insist on harmonious following, and resulting unity, of one's center of gravity with that of the horse. By always remaining in a lack of opposition to the horse's shifting center of gravity, we temporarily deny ourselves the capacity to aid for changes. Rather, we temporarily commit ourselves to maintaining the status quo by allowing the horse to initiate while we follow. By insisting on the harmonious union of our center of gravity with the horse's, we become friendly insiders to his motion. By following the horse consistently, even in his rhythmic irregularities and abrupt directional changes, we can convey partnership. This attitude is analogous to dancing. We influence our dancing partners imperceptibly in the most arduous tempo changes, shifts in balance, speed and direction.

Much like a leader of the dance influences his partner harmoniously with subtleties, so must riders influence their following partner, the horse. This cannot come about unless unity of purpose is established by both the leader and the follower seeking the unity of their balance.

Often young horses or 'green' horses will loose their balance as soon as the rider mounts. Better gymnasticized horses will continue to struggle for balance in a more sophisticated manner. Yet every discerning rider is aware of the precarious nature of the common balance that must exist between horse and rider. Good riders will perpetually shepherd and maintain good balance and will harmoniously share the center of gravity with their horse.

Young horses often drift sideways, (hence my admonition that not all sideways movement is a half-pass!) and alternately slow and hasten their strides as their centers of gravity ceaselessly shift. The loss of balance, of course, is commensurate with the physical weakness, lack of athletic skills for self carriage and fear of or inattention to the rider. The rider has not yet been recognized as the partner who can solve problems and who secures a life in the comfort zone. We have to convince the young horse of our abilities in that direction, and the best way to proceed is to propose a partnership in motion. When we can induce a dance between horse and rider, we cease to command him from the outside. Instead, we pretend to become partial to his motions and even his intentions, in the interest of gaining a partner and not an opponent in the horse. To a partner of purpose and motion, any horse may surrender the propellant energy of his haunches and lend his back for carriage; that is the obedience we covet.

Once he has submitted, the horse will allow the leader of the dance, the rider, to control and guide him in a choice of speed and direction initially and later to control his rhythm and precise patterning. Of course, engagement will gradually follow as communications, from horse to rider and from rider to horse, become more sophisticated. To move exactingly straight along the walls of the dressage arena, and bent in each corner, will take a horse trained to Grand Prix performance. Prior to that, compromise in the exactness of the

Two great men in majestic progress with comfort and confidence great enough to allow both of them to turn for a view to the side. The Renaissance has given remarkable emphasis on proportion to these two monuments which transcends the physical appearance. These monuments are equally imbued with a physical beauty born of a sense of proportion and of an emotional and intellectual simplicity that make these men elegant. Proud but not haughty, elegant without opulence, tranquil without being dull, and majestic without greed, these monuments are a splendid commentary on the most noble in the human spirit.

Incidentally, both horses show the flexion of that muscle in the neck which is still the indispensable element in the horse's connecting from hocks through to the bridle. One more relaxed and slightly bent right, the other with the highest posture possible without tension, both horses are models of the result of many years of correct schooling. Whatever gives cause to these rider's pride, I would add to it their horsemanship.

pattern must be made in the interest of the athletic essentials, a properly stretched horse moving straight with evenly loading haunches.

Obviously, confronting young horses with arguments about disciplined patterns is premature. They can oblige only at the expense of compromising suppleness. When prematurely 'forged exact,' patterns are stress-producing on the muscular-skeletal delivery of the horse. However, patterns must remain important gymnastic training tools, like weights in a gymnasium, and evaluative devices for the assessment of the horse's athletic progress.

2. As the horse presents opportunities, one should take advantage of them. When the horse initiates acceptable actions, the rider should promote them. This will improve the horse's confidence in his rider's guidance.

For instance, by turning on a diagonal, a horse may offer a longer, more floating stride. The rider should not merely permit such an initiative by harmonizing with it, but rather should encourage the horse to *maximize the delivery* of his own ideas! Opportunistic riding of this kind fosters progress and inspires the horse's confidence in his rider. The horse can learn that when he does things well he remains unopposed. The individuality, character and special talents of each horse are our most valuable assets. Horses should be encouraged to display initiative and enjoy our acquiescence to them. After all, we must always be flexible to change training plans in an instant. No good rider ever carries out his planned training program for the day; the ability to correctly improvise is the foundation of correct training strategy.

If a horse is often, or always, corrected when he volunteers initiative, the rider will break his spirit. A horse cannot perceive or conceive of a programmed partnership that does not tolerate spontaneity. When we drive for an extended trot, the horse might strike an unexpected canter. Take advantage of this opportunity to improve the canter. It does not matter that the canter was not in the planned program at that moment. It is more important that it happens to be what we now have. So work on it! Avoid admitting to a horse, especially a green one, that you made a mistake. Rather, pretend that you wanted whatever he happened to do.

Chances are, anyway, that you may have inadvertently asked for whatever you now consider a 'mistake.' Often our signals are muddled or improper in their clarity and intensity. Why shouldn't the horse misread them? We must not blame the horse for something that we may have caused or even provoked.

Horse-initiated actions that are not dangerous should be considered as potentially good, desirable and useful, and therefore welcome. For the continued progress both in mental partnership and physical development, pursue the horse's ideas with encouragement.

Consistency is the key to good training. Therefore reward by at least harmonizing with any motion that the horse volunteers that is supportive of athletic development. Riders best develop their "listening" abilities while remaining alert to opportunities the horse presents.. Acceptance of happenstance also builds rider humility by admitting that even a horse can suggest valuable training strategies.

The most commonly reported opportunistic occurrences include flying changes, prompted by fear, surprise, fatigue or adjustment of balance; the first step of piaffe from frustration with the collected walk or while in transition; the passage from excitement, displaying dominance or even resisting sudden transitions between extended and collected gaits.

3. School to do things correctly. Two wrongs will never make one right. If something is performed incorrectly by the horse, no punishment will correct it. For a horse can only understand corrective guidance that shows him *what* to *do,* not the kind that shows only *what not to do!*

Usually the rider is to blame for the wrong a horse has done. Misunderstanding or inability to perform what has been asked for can prompt the horse to deliver the incorrect results. The rider must patiently assess the causes of non-delivery and school the horse through to understand how it can be done well. Show repeatedly, patiently and pleasantly how to do it correctly. Punitive, illogical, unreasonable riding will not teach a horse anything.

For instance, if a horse is rushing, do not jam him into a sliding halt by chucking him in the teeth. Instead, patiently slow him down, hinting of an approach to a walk on a loose rein. When he does slow, lower his neck and poll to put that slow motion through his topline. Repeat as often as necessary, as with all good medicine. Carefully monitor right and wrong behavior. Reinforce the former with rewards and the latter with painless forms of 'punishment.'

4. Ask for, rather than command, performance. Riding is based on a continuum of activities between extreme permissiveness to extreme punishment and rudeness. Along this punishment and reward continuum, there is a definite breaking point where punishment stops and reward begins. The lowest level of reward is the absence of pain, often as simple as harmony.

Asking for nothing new, accepting the status quo can communicate our pleasure in the horse's contentment. After all, every new command is a mild punishment; in asking for a new thing, we disturb the horse's inertia, both mental and physical. Changes are more fatiguing, this aiding for something new, as opposed to harmonizing with existing performance is, indeed, the minimum punishment in the conceptual continuum.

Therefore riders must ask and not command the horse to do anything. Sophisticated riders on precisely trained horses may appear to dictate and command to a push-button horse that just loves discipline. What superficial nonsense! The instant willingness of the horse to respond to the imperceptible suggestions of a sophisticated rider is the very by-product of years of harmonious familiarity and the resultant attitude of joy to please. The partnership, when right, is not sadomasochistic (the most immature of relationships) but love-based (the most selflessly mature).

Riders should ask the horse to do things in harmony, and in the horse's time, because it is his body being borrowed for the athletic efforts. The mind of the rider can wait, and hold in check impatience and impertinence. The horse is a calendar; ask and wait. The horse will deliver when he is ready.

I hope to have contributed some logical, systematic thoughts to my plea for the gradual, harmonious training of the horse. After all, we should ride for the joy of the process of harmonious communications between horse and rider. If, coincidentally, the horse is ready to perform what we seek, we should consider it a gift from the horse. A process knows no end, has no terminus and is never finished by arrival. Once the process 'arrives,' it is eliminated. There is no joy in deadline. The desire to *be* something is ego-oriented and useless to the horse. Strive to *do* something instead! Do not seek arrival but enjoy the process of getting there. We can only quest for our equestrian ideals. We never attain them, as witnessed by no 100 % score on any one's dressage test. We should be happy to approximate the standards of the ideals we uphold and to do that without causing pain and anguish to the horse. Brutality begins where knowledge ends. Ignorance and compulsion appear simultaneously.

9
"On The Bit"

There are a few misleading terms in equestrian terminology and possibly the two most harmful are "the horse on the bit" and "rein back."

I have found that these terms cause images and suggest activities which are misleading riders in their pursuit of the knowledge inherent in classical horsemanship.

I will limit myself to offering some conceptual alternatives to the term, "the horse on the bit." In an effort to make the true meaning of this unfortunate phrase clearer, I will repeatedly rephrase its meaning. Several alternative, descriptive sentences might help one understand a conceptual definition.

Here is what we are aiming and looking for when referring to "the horse on the bit":

1. To connect the energy created by the horse's haunches (its propellant locomotion) through a stretched and elevated spine (topline) to his mouth, which must be allowed to softly seek contact with the bit.

2. The bit should be passively offered by the rider for the horse's seeking of its contact for his benefit. He can "read the rider's mind" on the bit regarding the recycling of his

energies. Namely, the rider can monitor how much energy from the haunches is used to magnify the horse's motion into extension or collection, and how much must be retained for the maintenance of the horse's carriage or posture.

3. To bridge the flexing hind leg joints to the navigational and balancing forehand. The relationship of the rider's energizing the haunches and his moderating this energy supply through the reins, which are extensions of his seat, tells the horse how to balance his extensions or collections through proper carriage. This allows the horse to*carry* his rider forward rather than just move onward.

4. To use the yielding activities of the reins and the bit in order to encourage the relaxation and stretching of the horse's musculature. This will facilitate the horse's ability to absorb the concussion of the impact on the ground throughout his entirety and, therefore, without trauma to his joints and muscles.

5. To use the yielding of the reins in order to encourage the "deepening" of the horse's flexion of the topline. That is the lowering of the "middle neck" and with it, of course, the poll, in order to raise the back yet higher. The rider driving towards yielding reins will make the "hoop" on which he sits rounder and more resilient and softly swinging.

6. To move the horse through his entirety means that all tensions and blocking of mobility caused by harsh hands, should be avoided. Only a horse moving through his entirety can avoid traumatic impact with the ground and give the rider access to his haunches.

7. The hands and the reins should neither inhibit the horse's strides, nor confine his neck. Instead, one ought to offer a soft and steady hand, independent of the balancing activities of the rider, to a confident horse that is stretching

The soldier ready for battle. His courage doubled by that of his horse. Maneuvering as one, they both know their moves in the midst of their enemies.

Indeed, much of classical equitation is rooted in the refinements of human control over a trained horse for purposes of successful battle. The ultimate goal was to develop and refine the horse's natural movements most relevant for use in war. Defending his rider, contributing to the rider's fierceness and force over his enemies, the horse made the difference in the outcome. Saving the life of his rider, the horse grew into an historical hero. Sharing the dares and victories of centuries of contest and combat.

Only when welded in a physical union could action of purpose follow. The privilege of the rider to guide the obedient powers of his horse was earned by the adhesiveness of his seat. Here one can visually understand that the adhesive seat refers to unrelenting contact of a draped rider over his horse whose contact areas always remain adhesive. The immensity of action is not weakening the physical unity but is born of it. For without the rider's confident affinity to his horse, no action so daring could ever follow. Both horse and rider trust that they will not lose each other. They will either prevail or perish together.

towards the bit and seeks an even contact with it.

8. To know that what we feel in the hand is symptomatic of the activities of the haunches. Therefore, the hands can usually be corrected by controlling the haunches, rather than the forehand, or worse, the mouth.

9. To understand that sometimes stretching must be initiated from the front by yielding the reins when it depends on improved relaxation of the horse's musculature; other times, stretching must be encouraged by activating or driving the haunches, energizing or strengthening the horse's spine.

10. To understand that even the highest degree of collection is based on the horse's muscles and spine being fully stretched. In fact, the "tautness of the bow" in the horse's topline is keener in collection than in extension. However, a rider should never attempt to "collect" a horse by compacting or inhibiting the horse through his neck by too firm a contact on the bit.

11. A horse must be allowed the freedom to carry his neck according to the dictates of the engagement of his haunches. That is the meaning of self-carriage and it must be based on utter freedom from restrictive rein contact. The rider must never seek more contact than the horse does. The bit belongs to the horse!

12. To know that contact with the horse's mouth felt by the rider should never, except in emergencies, be a matter of force. So long as there is weight, or force, that must be held or sustained by the rider, the horse is not in self-carriage and the contact is incorrect, eliminating all its beneficial attributes. *Self-carriage is a necessity during all stages of training,* and it is accomplished by years of training.

13. To know that engagement of the haunches can only occur when driving produces energy that is allowed or invited to

travel through the horse's stretched and elevated topline. That engagement has many elements, among them acute flexion of the horse's joints; flexing or rotating of the lumbo-sacral joint to "tuck the pelvis under," and increased flexion in the horse's lower back. All these physical changes result in the horse's ability to use his limbs and posture more efficiently for the lengthening and collecting of strides.

14. Only the correct harmony between driving and receiving forces of the rider can negotiate genuine submission, because submission is nothing more than the horse's voluntary surrender of his haunches to the rider and the soft carriage of his swinging back, which propels his rider in comfort.

You can see that there is no way to rephrase the succinct term "on the bit" with another three words. One must instead trust that all "terminus technicus" in any art and science will be correctly understood by all its experts.

Those who know their art will not misinterpret even poor terminology because they will distinguish between its superficial message and its real meaning. Proportionate to ignorance is the ability to take literally the sad advice to "put the horse on the bit."

It is therefore important to know that there is "no neutrality" in classical horsemanship. One is either contributing to the horse's well-being by rehabilitation, restoration or gymnastic development, or one is breaking him down. There is never anything "in neutral" or on "hold" or ready to "just wait a minute." Horsemanship is always working with full commitment towards benefit or harm.

The "rein back" is a misnomer because it refers to backing a horse which, indeed, should be done but without pulling on the reins! The term "rein back" suggests that the rider should pull his horse back to force him to step back from the stress and pain in his mouth. Nothing is further from the correct way a rein back should be executed.

To step back with a horse one prepares him with a straight, four square and well balanced halt. The rider prepares his position by draping his legs somewhat back from the "on the girth position" to the so-called "outside leg's canter position." Usually only the outside leg is slightly behind the position of the inside one, in the so-called "canter position." This position is necessary not just for cantering but also for all times when bending the horse laterally.

For stepping back, however (and for Piaffe), both legs push back to the "canter position" and drape the horse's sides at the identical place, parallel, on both his sides. Care must be taken that the heels remain well below the elevated toe, maintaining that important flexion in the ankles which stretches the calves to provide the driving aids. This leg position will help keep the horse straight between the "corridor" of rein and leg aids. It will also slightly lighten the seat bones, easing the torso pressure from forward driving to an attitude that instead, suggests an "opening of the gates" for back-stepping progression.

The rider's torso must be firmly unified into an isometric, meaningful "cabinetry" which can facilitate the "passive resistance" in the reins. Hands should remain as low as possible, fists close together and very stable.

The horse is asked with the rider's legs (calves) and *not* the spur, to move on. His response should be a sense of forward energy. However, sensing the passive resistance of the reins which are connected to the torso and finding the "forward gate" to progression therefore closed, he will naturally opt to step back where the lighter seat has "opened a new door towards backing."

When the horse takes the very first step backward, the rider should immediately confirm that the horse correctly understood the request by yielding slightly through the reins. The

The two noble renderings of horses' heads are somewhat abstract. They were sculpted more than a thousand years apart from one another. Yet they both present horses with discernible personal characteristics and attributes. The turning of their heads allows their personalities to emerge as they pay attention to events that fascinate them.

pressure for driving should remain constant with both legs. Neither alternating, nor pulsating or kicking, leads to much good. Restless, sometimes not-contacting legs can cause the horse to stall or go crooked. Steady legs, positioned well stretched and back will facilitate both good driving and ability to respond to crookedness by quickly straightening the horse.

The lightening of contact upon the first correct response of the horse and the steadily driving legs will assure even, calm, continuous progress backwards. When the desired number of strides back have been performed, the rider's legs should slide forward, maintaining pushing contact. This will drop the seat bones down to the heavier, forward driving position and allow the torso to lean back enough to thrust the pelvis forward. The hands once again yield. With these harmoniously synchronized actions, the horse will progress forward immediately following his backing, without a loss of rhythm.

Overflexing, resistance, curling the haunches to one side, hurrying backwards, plunging forwards, opening the mouth, pinning the ears: all reveal incorrect controls by the rider. A confused, misguided horse will not back stride with an appearance of forward zest and its companion feeling of going forward again the moment the rider requests it.

The "rein back" is not done in the footfall of the walk. It is executed by moving the diagonal pairs of legs alternately, much like at the trot. But here, of course much slower, akin to the tempo of a walk and without suspension. However, the horse's feet should lift well off the ground and not scrape it. The lumbar back should tuck, the lumbo-sacral joint should flex, the croup should lower, the pelvis tilt forward. The horse becomes stronger, more collected and learns the skills of lowering the haunches. Because the exercise is so important I wanted to emphasize that it utterly precludes any pulling on the reins. The only stress that might develop on the rein at the beginning stages of schooling this movement will be the stress created by the horse feeling his way against the passive resistance of the rider. Here again, we must not talk to the horse's mouth. We merely allow him to differentiate between using the rider's driving energies for stepping back, after he has calmly found the "front doors closed," denying him the usual forward progression.

As all exercises, the stepping back of a horse should be taught calmly, gradually and with frequent rewards for correct responses. First one or two steps should be enough and generously rewarded. Even at its most sophisticated, one ought not ask for more than six strides backing.

10
Engagement on the Aids

Bringing the horse to the aids is primarily done by the driving leg aids, and only secondarily with the concurring seat and derivative hand aids, as they all work together as a system. *The horse cannot be engaged through the hands.* This is not because I think it wrong, but because it is physiologically impossible. This is not just matter of style, emphasis, method or taste. It is a fact of objective physiological data.

When the horse is properly on the aids, the neck will arch and the poll will flex as part of the total longitudinal flexion. On top of the horse's spinal column, running the entire length, is the cervical ligament. That ligament should be fully stretched at all times. When it is fully stretched, not only will its elasticity and therefore swinging activity increase, but it will also elevate the horse's back or spinal column. To elevate the back, one should "pull down" the cervical ligament at both its ends; that is, have the horse tuck his haunches under and push his neck forward and down simultaneously

That is why just showing the way to the ground to the horse, in effect lowering his head, is not enough without at the same time driving his haunches under him; the cervical ligament, and with it the back, will fully stretch and elevate only when both ends of it are approaching the ground.

When the haunches engage more (and often the whip must be used to insist on it), the horse's biceps femoris muscles visibly press the stifle farther forward and upward, a major function, while lifting the hocks higher in their rotation, a lesser function. The muscles, running on the back side of the horse's rump, are observable at the walk, trot or canter during the action that tucks the haunches under: they pull the back end of the cervical ligament tight. Because it is attached to the horse's skull, the front of the ligament can be stretched simultaneously by riding the horse's head forward and down. Without this simultaneous drawing down of the front and back end of the cervical ligament and the surrounding musculature, the horse is physiologically incapable of carrying the rider properly and developing gymnastically.

When the back has been elevated, the horse can balance himself and relax those muscles that are furthering effortless locomotion and carriage. Thus, the correctly stretched horse (and remember, this is attained by a driving rider) will hang his head from the muscles running at the upper sides of his neck between the withers and the seventh cervical or one of the first thoracic vertebrae, the splenius primarily and the semispinalis capitis (located under the splenius) secondarily. The horse will then no longer need to support his head carriage by "shelving it up" with the muscles emitting from his chest (brachiocephalicus) and look as if he grew a goiter. Needless to say, on the longitudinally-flexed horse, also called "on the bit," all other muscles will also automatically relax and move with a great deal of flexion or stretching to create ample, loose, effortless locomotion. These relaxed muscles can be observed 'playing' in ripples under the fine summer coat of a correctly moving horse.

The greatest hindrance to driving the horse properly is from riders stiffening their legs. Gripping the horse with tight legs, pressing on his ribs inward, or tightly holding him with the heels, are all incorrect leg positions and deny aiding. Riding with the seam of the boots is a bad habit held over from times when the rider needed to grip in order to balance himself. Often "quietly elegant" legs are confused with tightly gripping leg positions. The horse cannot monitor tight legs as aids and will sour to the pressure, which he will interpret as another "necessary evil."

Weight on the horse's sides will be tolerated much like weight in the saddle, but gripping legs never modulate and therefore never "converse." In human terms, tight gloves do not communicate what gently squeezing hands can. Tight legs also induce pain and discomfort much like tight shoes. In fact, with the passing of time, the pain induced by both tight shoes, for humans, and tightly gripping legs, for horses, will sharply increase and approach the intolerable level.

Some riders' legs are positioned so as to rub backwards and upwards onto the horse's sides, with toes out and down, which locks in the stirrups, heels pulled up and pressing backwards. The opposite is necessary: relaxed legs, deep heel position and pushing action on the horse's sides downward and forward. Easily said, but how do we do it?

Put your stirrups out toward your toes; that gives you a longer foot, enabling your heels to drop. Only with dropped heels can you give supple strength to your calf, with which you must aid, rather than with the heels. A short foot, with stirrups at the ball of the foot or locked further in towards the ankle cannot rotate properly to give pushing aids.

To use the calves and not the heels, the ankles must be relaxed and rotating. When your legs are back where they belong, with the toe behind the knee, you can slowly turn the toes inward, followed by lowering of the heels. This pushes the toes slightly outward, followed by turning the toes inward again. The feeling in walk and canter is slow and rhythmic, pushing forward and down on the horse's sides. In the trot, the tempo is much faster, and on a green horse some bouncing of the calf off his barrel is all right. But later, one wants a smooth undulation of the calves without their leaving the horse's barrel completely.

To build skill and feeling, you should aid the horse with your toes by circling the toes inward toward the horse's body. You should not touch the horse with your toes. But by

Palatial buildings in the most excessively decorated aesthetic era, the Baroque, were even topped by running and leaping horses. Nowhere to go, yet ready to tumble from great heights, horses and people take flight in sculpture and fancy. No mere architectural building could cajole the emotions that would make it so significant without the assistance of the wonderful horses, magnificently animated, so close to the roof of their world.

bouncing the toes inward, you will succeed in suppling your ankles and actually aiding with your calves! To ignore calf aids, the only pushing aids possible, and an insistence on aiding with the heels instead is the ruin of many riders.

Rhythmically repetitious, forward, pushing aids are the only legitimate driving aids. Of course they also coordinate the proper functioning of the muscles of the buttocks that partake in driving. Such aids are effortless and feel light; they burn no calories and the horse reacts to their companionship with lively gaits. While learning correct driving aids or teaching them to the horse, the frequent and consistent use of the whip is necessary. The horse must react to these rhythmically light and harmonious aids, and if he forgets to react, you must "jump a spark to his batteries" with your cable/whip! The whip serves as the spark that connects the rider's mind and will to his horse's mind and consequently gains submission. When the whip is used, the legs should simultaneously aid so that the horse learns to associate the leg pressure with the whip. It is much better to settle the attention-to-the-aids issue firmly early on than to nag at the horse for fourteen years!

Never forget that an effective aid is not exhausting to the rider and not souring to the horse. Never forget that the horse is capable of flicking a fly of his skin and therefore can tune in to the lightest aids *if that is what you teach him.* Do not forget that the horse can and should always pay attention to the rider while working, but should also be given frequent rest periods. The horse's ears should not listen by pointing forward, but should be relaxed and slightly slack toward the rider in a position of submissive listening. His eyes should not focus forward or roll sideways in observation of all others but should look somewhat relaxed as if in a daze with an inward vision. As soon as the horse is off the aids, tune him back with a whip!

We can ride neither forward nor sideways by physically dislocating horses with force. That is, we cannot push them around. Regardless of how much power you use, you cannot force the horse to do anything. No amount of strength can compel the horse to do anything. The simple reason for this is that the rider is not on his own legs. You can no more force a horse in any direction by physical muscle power than your ear lobes can force you to change your course or increase impulsion. Thus, muscle power and force will not ride the horse for you, only aids will, and they might as well be light and harmonious.

The horse has the neurological aptitude to react to very slight stimuli. He has the mental aptitude to perceive for a sustained period of time very mild stimuli and to differentiate between them. He has an excellent memory. Force and power will only stiffen the rider. Sensitive aids will result in exquisite communications. If a horse pulls on you, remember that it takes two to pull! If you "un-pull," yield one rein at a time, the horse cannot and will not pull. Horses will learn anything. They will learn to gymnasticize with you on light communications just as easily as they will learn to do the same by harsh communications.

To increase the horse's attention to the leg aids, two-track exercises are the most valuable. For when inducing a crossing of one hind leg by your leg action on the same side, you communicate to the horse that an action way up on his ribs intends to yield results way down at his hooves. Two-track movements have terrific gymnastic value. Nothing else "brings the horse onto the aids" more firmly than obedience to the two-track aids.

To build the horse from behind is no idle notion. It is a physiologically predetermined, compulsory position. Remember, it can be done as soon as you succeed in gaining the horse's attention to your forward driving aids. As soon as the horse accepts your legs without rushing, and instead demonstrates "staying power." tolerance to the leg's conversation, he should produce upon the lightest inducement results of slower but larger rotation of the haunches. Nothing can develop from the head backwards. It is your job to teach him your legs; tolerate no compromise. The way is forward and upward in a slow rhythm.

The alternative method for collection is, of course, through *longitudinal engagement* activity. First of all, you must feel the rate of progression of your horse, and harmonize with it. It is most evident in the trot, but the same applies to the walk or canter. Go along, follow, move with, dance along, passively agree to feel what he supplies from the haunches. This is a short but diagnostic period during which you are a listener monitoring that which the horse offers in the concept areas of relaxation, submission, and neck fully forward. Some of the shoulder action of the horse is kept in reserve, not allowing the horse to fully extend in the shoulders. Therefore, the medium trot is ample in length, but not fully extended to the horse's utmost stretching ability. The taller neck position, and taller but shorter use of shoulder action, composes the medium trot into a very energetic, elegant movement that is engaged behind but produces height of steps and a distinct lightening of the forehand, in effect bouncing the withers up and lifting the knees higher.

The medium trot is the "bread and butter" exercise on the way to Grand Prix. Without the medium gaits, the proper muscular development producing the proper skeletal rotation just cannot develop. The Grand Prix is born by work in the medium gaits, with ample mileage spent staying with it.

The 20-meter circle is a useful gymnastic tool which, being a continuous line, allows the perpetual flow of motion rather than the corner-to-straight rearrangements of the horse's balance and rider's aids. To the medium gaits' development the sense of *perpetual motion* is highly important. Riders often feel that too much driving work at medium gaits is detrimental. Remember, though, that just a century or so ago in Paris, London, Vienna and the world's other metropolises, horses were medium trotting across cities, carrying their passengers to dinners, dentists, theaters, shopping, maintaining the pace for miles, hour after hour, on pavement, day after day. Your horse can do it too.

The medium trot has the distinct signature of great engagement and impulsion in the quarters, stepping deeply under, combined with slow and elevated motion of forehand as if to "wait" for the arrival of the haunches. That relative restraint in the forehand in relation to the keenness of the haunches defines that wonderful forward yet bouncing, upward motion that gives the feeling of the horse rising in front of the thighs and sinking behind the seat bones. Only through that combination of elongation and elevation of strides can medium gaits develop.

Of course, the passage is born out of the medium trot. Both the strength and the skills needed by the horse for passage comes forth from medium trot work. Once the horse is ready for it, often a bold half-halt from a medium trot can make the horse collect into passage.

The medium compared to full extended trot can forestall any mistake on the horse's part in misinterpreting driving aids for speed or shifting the weight onto the forehand.

I hope you will begin to engage your horses by using the three fundamental methods I have recommended here; put him on your aids and teach him what your legs mean, and use the bending and two-track movements. To mobilize him and confirm his balance, use transitions from longer to shorter strides; to stabilize his tempo and put mileage on his muscular development and skeletal proficiency, ride the circle at the medium gaits.

11
Developing a Correct Seat

What is the reason behind all those requirements for the rider's seat?

Without a correctly sitting rider the horse cannot move without pain or discomfort. The absence of this discomfort signals the beginning of cooperation through which we can gain the horse's trust in us and attention to our desires. Only a correctly seated rider can apply the aids effectively. By the combination of being a pleasant weight and communicating properly, we may achieve the desired athletic development in our horse.

As in most athletic endeavors, the rider must develop the seemingly contradictory qualities of relaxation and strength. Relaxation allows horse and rider to harmonize, not only by virtue of absence of discomfort or pain, but by finding pleasure in moving through space in cooperative unity. With appropriate strength in the necessary areas of the rider's musculature, he can communicate through his aids to direct the horse's athletic development. That development is based on the ability to ride the horse in gymnastically helpful patterns and in an authentically appropriate frame or bodily situation. In the process, both horse and rider learn balance, their muscles are suppled, and their joints elasticized.

The balance of the rider in the saddle is the first step to accomplish. As long as the rider fears falling off, or even just fears losing balance by slipping, relaxation cannot be expected. When losing balance we instinctively tighten many muscle groups, the wrong ones, in the hope that sheer strength and gripping will secure us in the saddle. Lungeing by an expert, providing the rider with many hours in the saddle without having to concentrate on controlling the horse, gives a sense of safety to the rider and allows instruction to improve his balance. At first the rider should help his balance by holding the pommel or a neck strap. The rider can then gradually give up the gripping with his hands for safety for increasingly longer periods, and this will grow gradually independent of the necessity to hold. Soon, an initial balance will be established. But further refinement is necessary, so when the rider has stopped slipping in the saddle at the basic gaits, he can begin exercises that involve moving various parts of his body independently.

An *independently balanced rider* emerges through the long process of exercises *suppling and stretching,* done at the three basic gaits. Since they enhance independent control of specific parts of the rider's body, they are indispensable in enabling the rider to assume control over his horse and begin rudimentary but meaningful application of the aids. The exercises should involve every part of the body, literally from the toes (uncurl them for heaven's sake!) to the eyelids (close them often).

An equestrian becomes a rider as soon as he has acquired a balanced and independent seat. Now he may be allowed to

Two monuments with horses at halt but their attention diverted from their riders. Both riders gesturing similarly with their arms and their attentions are diverted from their horses. The monuments, created at least a century apart, convey the same ideas. Horses and riders can divert their attentions from one another momentarily, provided there is full trust between them.

take control of his horse. Prematurely allowing control of the horse by the novice rider accounts for terrible habits of seat and aids that may never be completely corrected, only mellowed. Also, the psychological effects of being victimized by the horse who soon discovers that the unbalanced, tense, and ineffective rider is easy prey for frolicking and so uncomfortable a burden that he should be gotten rid of, can remain detrimental to the rider forever.

Now let me call your attention to some particulars concerning the rider's seat and aids. These are the skills most often lacking in many riders' performances. Unfortunately, to physically adjust and make proper a rider's seat is not possible in print, but takes personal instruction.

The rider's head should never be tipped or inclined sideways, with the chin to one side. The neck should be back as if leaning against a head support in a car: the neck has vertebrae that must remain part of a straight and upright spinal column. The neck muscles should be relaxed, so that the rider is able to look sideways without affecting his functions elsewhere. Obviously, we ought to look around in both flatwork and jumping. A good exercise is to turn the head from side to side slowly until the chin is placed over the collar bone but remains high.

The shoulder blades should be straightened and tightened to make them lie flat in the musculature; not as visible butterfly wings—they should only have an inch or so between them. This lifts the rib cage up and the chest out, insuring good breathing and a straight spine. The rider must concentrate on correct body posture constantly, including when dismounted, even while driving a car. Shoulder blades flat into the back! The upper arms must hang in a relaxed fashion from shoulder joints that are back and down. Imagine that the elbows are weighted with lead. The great mistake is to stretch the arms forward, thereby rounding the shoulders and rendering the chest concave.

Do not ever arch or hollow the lower back and thereby stiffen it. That horrible position nullifies the functions of the lower back, which, in my opinion, *is where riding is!* Riders who press the crotch down, pushing the hips ahead of seat bones, and slant the lower abdomen over the pommel, have never felt what riding is. They "limb ride" and eliminate even the vaguest possibility of feel, never know where the horse's quarters are, and cannot sense the condition of the back muscles, which they pound stiff by that position. Such riders can only accelerate with legs and brake with hands. With a hollow back, the rider's body cannot be used as the "transformer" of the energy fed from the haunches, absorbed through the seat, and returned to the horse's mouth forward by the lower arms in an appropriately altered fashion.

The rider's thighs should remain flat on the sides of the saddle and should be relaxed (unless in jumping position or rising the trot) but stretched from his hip, so that the knees stay low and back. To create this very important deep knee and long stretched contact situation, the best exercise is to ride the trot without stirrups. It will also vastly improve the rider's balance, even eliminating falling off!

The stretching of the calf muscles (ankle extensors) and the ability to contract those around the shin bone (ankle flexors), producing the heels down, toes up position, are crucial for stable, quiet, strong, and appropriate driving and bending aids. Without properly formed and used calves, there is simply no effective riding! A common fault is that riders wanting "dressage," often attempt to ride "that style" by lengthening their stirrups by four notches. Wrong! The rider *must earn* the long stirrups *gradually* as he stretches his muscles and sinews: his legs "get longer" from the hip to the heel and *necessitate* the lengthening stirrups *one hole at a time* as this development takes place. So start with *very short* stirrups, rise or stand in your knees until they are worked down and back, while the heels are forced to sink down and back as the stirrup irons insist on keeping your toes higher than the heels. Then, in sitting trot and canter, keep trying in short stirrups, always taking care that the knee remains pressed back and down: *bend your knees!* The feeling is similar to going down on your knees in church. It takes concentration and perpetual readjustment of the slipping knees and lower legs: back and down with them while keeping the heels as the rider's lowest points.

The upper arms should *hang vertically downward* (not to be extended forward), and the elbows should be well bent and should feel weighted. Do not flare the elbows away from the rib cage nor push them into your ribs. Start by hanging the arms straight down, then bend at the elbows, with nearly horizontal lower arms. Put your two fists close together in front of your abdomen. Adjust the length of the reins so that you can hold them in that relaxed position. There should be both relaxation and tranquillity in the arm muscles, and a steadiness at the shoulder and elbow joints. Without these qualities there can be no independent hands; the rider's hands will jolt, jar, dance, and jiggle around.

The wrists should be straight: that is, the back of the rider's hand should be on the same plane, a straight continuum, as his forearm. If you assume this correct position, the large joints of your fingers should touch when you press your fists together. The hooked wrists, bent out so that they can touch on the inside is stiff and incorrect, as are hollow wrists that make two sets of the knuckles in the fingers.

All fingers should be closed all the time: a complete fist should be made, with all the fingertips lined up in one row in the middle of the palm. Open fingers do not demonstrate light hands! They are dreadfully wrong and even dangerous, for such a rider will constantly lose some of the rein and will have to repeatedly readjust. The contact will be upset, altered and restless. Because many riders do not learn initially to ride with closed fingers and a closed fist, at higher levels they keep losing the contact with the snaffle and will remain holding only the curb bit, thereby overflexing and tensing their advanced horses. The end of the thumbs should point down into the sharp angle formed by the large joint of the bent forefinger. *The pressure of the reins should be there, the friction for holding a steady contact produced by the thumb pressure holding the reins tightly against the forefinger.*

These suggestions should take a while to carry out, and I wish you fast progress in acquiring these skills.

12
The Use of Hands and Reins

Let us review the "direct reins" as they should be:

1. Fingers closed, fists closed with isometric muscular coordination.

2. The first knuckle of the thumb the highest point of the fist, yet the tip of both thumbs tilted towards each other.

3. If the fists were to touch each other, the knuckles of the forefinger and the middle finger should both touch the same two on the other hand, in order to be at the correct angle.

4. The outside of the lower arm is a straight continuation of the plane of the back of the hand, creating the straight wrist, without which the horse's mouth cannot be connected to the rider's seat activities.

5. The lower arm is raised or lowered, according to the developmental position of the horse's head and neck which

may be higher on more advanced horses. However, low hand carriage is to be encouraged throughout an equestrian career. Even on more advanced horses, the deeper the fists can sink, the greater the mastery of the haunches by the proper aids.

6. An obviously bent elbow and near vertical upper arm position completes the circle of coordination. On younger horses the upper arm should be vertical and the elbow sharply bent to ride *'with a long leather and a short arm'* and not the *'extended arm and short leather'* as one is invited by the horse to do. By then the isometric muscular coordination of the rider's arm and back muscles are so perfectly toned that with a somewhat forward elbow position tranquillity, steadiness, sensitivity, and contact can be

These beautiful horses have enough energy left to frolic and play, beyond their duties to pull while swimming. Vigor, independence, power and nobility are all there in all four horses, yet beyond these qualities, each remains an essentially different individual. The Renaissance genius for admiration of individually unique qualities was obviously not confined to their view of humans. Horses were included in this remarkable distinction.

maintained on the proper level of being only an extension of the seat!

A horse should not be held back by the reins. Horses hindered by the rider's hands cannot engage their haunches properly, will work with discomfort and pain under stress, and throw tantrums. Limiting, inhibiting, stiff, disturbing rein contact will cause pain not only in the horse's mouth but also throughout his musculature, particularly in the neck muscles. Bad hands and ill-used reins can cause damage and deterioration of the joints in the haunches showing up in 'rein lameness' of various kinds, or uneven motion of the hind legs.

Equestrian history is full of stories about unmanageable horses tamed by kind use of the rider's hands, Alexander the Great being one such example. But no sensitive or sensible

The fearless horse that lunges through the placid pond is sized as if he were crossing an ocean. Poetic tranquility reflects in the pool, replacing agitation with confident vigor. This smallest of statues in the midst of the gigantic dimensions of the gardens still attracts the eyes and dominates the imagination without rival.

rider is void of the memories when a nervous or even threatening horse has been won over by some patting on the neck, stroking of the crest, or any activity which managed, even for a moment, to yield the reins and induce a cessation of pain and promote self-carriage.

The rider's hands should merely be the extensions of his seat and its influences and activities. Therefore, it is so important to ride with closed fists, straight wrists, and elbows held at near right angle and never with outstretched arms. Through the setting of these angles (shoulder relating to elbow, to wrist) at the arm joints, one can finally connect the horse's mouth to one's seat bones and affect the mouth with the seat, rather than with separated and therefore irrelevant hands.

The hand should either be passive resistant or yielding (on one side at a time: unilateral releases) much like the seat, which should either brace (resist) against the movement or follow (yield) and harmonize with it. With the combination of a retarding or bracing seat and a yielding, following, and suppling seat one can perform the crucial half-halts.

Again, correct hands should be the extension of the rider's seat, enabling him to experience the rewarding feeling that when a horse over-contacts (pulls), he pulls his rider more firmly down into his own back, thus making the rider deepen his seat and increasing its pressure, rather than what the horse hopes to achieve, namely lightening or dislodging the rider's seat. In essence, the horse should be able to 'ride himself' through the rider, who serves as an intermediary, similar to human gymnasts who can perform 'with themselves' through the intermediary of the parallel bars or a pair of rings hanging from the ceiling.

When a horse plunges into the rider's hands or begins to pull, the rider should not actively pull back. It takes two to pull and the contest will be won by the horse because he has the stronger muscles (his neck vs. your arm) and because you are on his back. Only a rider whose hands are synchronized with his seat can submit a horse to his aids. As a horse begins to take hold and pull, a good rider will be pulled down into the saddle, which will exert some pressure on the bit, via the rider's seat. The pressure then is actually exerted on the horse's back and spine, because the horse has failed to weaken the rider's seat by his pulling. Thus, the resistant horse is taught the most important lesson: if he pulls, he pulls on himself, not on his rider.

Of course, such effectiveness can only be achieved by the rider whose equitation is correct with a closed fist, a firm elbow position and straight shoulders blades. The rider's torso down to his seat bones should look and behave like the torso of a soldier standing at attention. Only the lower arms may not hang down but instead point forward to facilitate, with their extensions through the reins, the contact with the horse's mouth. This position puts the shoulder's weight *back and down* into the saddle, increasing it if the horse pulls against it. This isometrically sustained unity of arms and torso in their perpendicularly intercepting affect on the horse's spines creates the kind of seat which is secure by "the cabinetry" of the torso. For the seat of the rider is not only where the actual contact of the buttocks are. The seat emanates from the head-neck-shoulder and through the torso where its position and muscular activity communicate its effectiveness down into the horse's back. The buttocks are the surface contact through which the *seat* arrives, not emanates.

The use of the hands should not only be an extension of the activities of the seat but should *always be accompanied by driving.* There are no separate hand aids, per se, merely an *aiding system* which must reach the horse in completeness and unison with a strong coordination of all its elements. Thus, the horse should always sense consistency rather than confusion emanating from the rider, originating from several sources of influence. The rider should not only succeed in sitting on the horse but rather *seek to sit in the horse's motion.* Sitting with the horse's motion depends on the rider's skills to move in unity and balance with his horse. Inconsistency of aids could also be created by loose or shaky arms, bouncing elbows, or outstretched upper arms. Such bad habits result in rounded and stressed shoulders, with the hips tilted forward, causing ineffectiveness of the seat and reins. The weight is off the saddle; it is pressed down into the stirrup through stiff ankles with feet perched on the ball of the foot. Add misguided hands snapping the fingers open and shut in a valiant attempt to 'soften the contact' and 'engage the jaw' and a common picture of bad equitation is completed.

The primary function of the reins remains to invite and maintain the horse's longitudinal flexion *toward the bit,* and not to restrain or inhibit. The rein also has navigational functions, since it can directly influence the horse's forehand (shoulders, neck, and head) which is the horse's navigational equipment. Thus, the leading rein has direct navigational purposes.

To some extent the horse places the experienced rider's independent hands into positions of higher, lower, closer to the withers or somewhat distant from them, according to the horse's needs. The crucial thing to remember is that the hands, being directly connected to the seat, should at all times enhance the roundness or depth of the horse's flexion from the hocks through the entire top line to the poll.

As with all sciences, and in horsemanship as well, one can

offer information of varying degrees of detail. There have been many different rein positions discussed by experts and having been mainly descriptive, are very adequately and helpfully elaborated on. I find the simplest way is to discuss the three most basic hand-rein positions, on which all other seem to be refinements or elaborations.

Chart Summary of Hand Positions and Their Influences

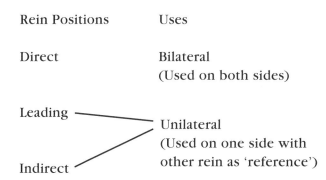

Rein Positions	Uses
Direct	Bilateral (Used on both sides)
Leading	Unilateral (Used on one side with
Indirect	other rein as 'reference')

The Direct Rein has the most thorough and direct influence on the haunches of the horse. He can feel in his mouth exactly what the rider is doing with his seat. The rein's direction remains as straight as possible between the rider's hips, through his elbows to the horse's mouth.

The direct rein allow the rider to feel the horse's mouth through the torso and allows the horse to sense in his mouth (through the reins) the depth of the rider's adhesive seat. The unity of seat and reins should be visible and the feeling is also conveyed to the horse that he can pull only on himself if he wants to pull, but he will never be able to pull the rider out of the saddle. One can also sense that when such a rider's seat follows the motion, his hands automatically contribute to the engagement by 'opening the doors of progression.' Thus direct reins actually participate in the driving.

The direct rein should be the most commonly used rein position. As the horse is advanced by the schooling rider in his mental and physical development, the rider earns the privilege of using a direct rein on both sides.

The Indirect Rein primarily increases the horse's positioning and bending of his neck, but also facilitates increased bending in the rest of his body. However, when misused by the rider by pulling, the rein can restrict and inhibit the rotation of the hock. The indirect rein's inhibitions will affect the hocks always on the same side where it has been pulled. This will cause the opposite of the desired effect—a decrease of bending and a stiffening and shortening of the strides.

The indirect rein can only be used on one side at a time. Never can we use both reins indirectly simultaneously because the direction of the indirect rein is from the horse's mouth towards the rider's chest or shoulder on the opposite side. Thus the power of the indirect rein is diagonally effective and is only unilaterally useful.

The indirect rein is very close to the horse's neck and even touches it. Slightly higher than the direct rein and much higher than the leading rein, it points 'across the withers and up.' The rotation of the wrist to the 'finger nails up' position ensures its minimal use and conveys the essence of its direction.

The Leading Rein is used in conjunction with the direct rein on the other side. The direct rein forms a triangle with the lead rein by distancing itself away from the horse's neck. It is the rider's lower arm, not the upper arm or elbow, that creates the distancing of the rein. It remains essential that the seat's influence is felt in the lead rein, via the intermediaries of a straight shoulder, a hanging upper arm and a steady elbow.

Also visible is the ideal straight line from the rider's elbow to the horse's mouth with the intermediary of the rein as an extension of the short human arm.

The leading rein is most often necessary on a young, green horse with balance problems and who, therefore, drifts. Drifting of the shoulders can best be counteracted by use of leading reins. The rider lowers his fist position, without straightening the elbow and disconnecting the seat bone, and forms a triangle with the reins by the placing of his fists relative to the horse's mouth. One fist, the direct rein, is placed close to the withers, or even resting on the pommel of the saddle, while the other sinks down and sideways even to the rider's thigh, away from the horse's neck, forming a triangle. If the one rein is not used as 'direct' but yields forward, the effect of the leading rein becomes nil. An incorrect position of the hands can make the rider look like a bicyclist holding the handle bars of his bike in a turn: wide hands with one fist ahead of the other. This is undesirable on horseback. Indeed, the effectiveness of the leading rein depends on the steadiness of the direct rein, which acts as a 'rein of reference.'

Regardless of the position in which the reins are used, the rider's hands should manage to yield with them appropriately, to encourage all rein uses as 'opening the door to progression.' and to encourage the increased rounding of the flexion that promotes the engagement of the haunches.

Only in emergencies should reins be used to inhibit. Otherwise the rider needs to tactfully use passive resistance, mostly through the seat, and that for as short a duration as possible. The rider must be careful during this passive resisting not to continue resisting but to yield as soon as possible. A prolonged use of restrictive rein and seat will only cause reluctance to forward movement.

13
Selecting Help for Classical Dressage Training

Many riders face a similar problem: How can one acquire a correct classical equestrian education? How can one even determine whether a teacher is educating in the right ways of horsemanship?

We all know that vast problems are often caused by shortages. We are experiencing a shortage of well-educated equestrian instructors. That is unfortunate for the sport. Those instructors who know their subject well and can effectively communicate it are in great demand. The rapidly growing number of riders interested in good instruction cannot access it easily.

If this shortage of knowledgeable instructors is causing trouble now, the future appears even worse. The attrition of the existing experts is inevitable, and so far efforts to educate their replacements are insufficient to meet the need for the quality and quantity of equestrian experts required.

Many riders know that great distances prevent them from

learning from superior teachers. Others may realize that while they occasionally take expert instruction from visiting clinicians, they can do this so seldom and, therefore, their education is not thorough and comprehensive. There are many riders who do not even know how to determine who the experts are. They cannot discern which instructors educate in the right manner and for the right objectives. They cannot fathom the depth or shallowness of an instructor's knowledge.

I think we would all feel troubled if we would have to become medical experts before choosing a knowledgeable doctor to treat us. Fortunately, however, the Medical Board licenses only experts for medical practice and only in their areas of expertise.

Yet equestrians must cope like African village dwellers might when facing a choice for medical help. Should they go to the tribal magician or to the doctor trained in Western medical institutions?

On returning from a battlefield, "The situation is desperate, but not hopeless...," an Austrian Imperial General is reputed to have reported to his Emperor in the nineteenth century. I think that this might be the case regarding the fate of our battle to retain classical horsemanship. We cannot "put the carriage in front of the horse" and become experts just in order to determine who the other experts are. We must take the necessary steps to make good equestrian instruction available.

In one's quest for good instruction, there are a number of things one can do to facilitate the process, including:

1. Ask about the background, schooling and qualifications of the instructor that you consider to be your mentor. Inform yourself about their expertise and use your logic to analyze

what their knowledge represents relative to your needs and goals. Ask others who have had experience with this instructor. Listen to their report on what they have learned and how that learning process took place. Ask what goals are emphasized by this instructor and what means are used to reach them. Ask for specifics as well as the generalities.

2. Develop your ability to judge the expertise of potential mentors by reading, attending seminars, courses, clinics and lectures.

3. Remember the expertise of instructors is highly individual and may be evaluated along an imaginary continuum from the most knowledgeable ones to utterly ignorant ones. The extreme examples would be imaginary because most instructor's knowledge may line up on a continuum between them. Certainly no one can know everything about any science, least of all about horsemanship, which is a somewhat subjective art based on experiences seeking harmony between two living, strong-willed and totally unlike creatures. However, the degrees of expertise can be likened to the scores given by dressage judges. Those who know "the right things" more or less score from five to ten. Those who are basically ignorant of the correct goals and admissible procedures to reach them score from four to zero. Select a teacher in the five to ten scoring range.

4. Expertise of the instructor is only part, but surely the most important and indispensable part of good instruction. In addition, teaching methods, techniques, even styles and manners, communication skills, and psychological insights all play important roles. Sometimes the most knowledgeable person may lack the communication skills and strategies to impart his knowledge for the recipient's benefit.

This is true in any science and art. The best physicians do not necessarily teach at medical schools. Each instructor has weaknesses and strengths. Areas of special emphasis, interest and knowledge are mixed with areas of disinterest, boredom and impatience. Instructing requires a sophisticated and complex ethical system. Good teachers in any field possess similar characteristics, including maturity and sophistication in the functions of synthesis and analysis. All good teachers seem to take their responsibilities seriously because they know they create believers and that is a privileged position. The ethics of teaching should include the desire to teach only one's expertise and not to verbalize beyond that.

5. Reading good books and articles may give you the finest guidelines in the selection of quality instruction. Good writings, including the FEI Rule Book, emphasize the most important and indispensable principles of classical equitation. Instructors not adhering to these should be avoided.

Some of the important principles of classical equitation include:

1. The correct equitation of the rider is more important in a lesson than the training needs of the horse. An inadequate rider attempting to train a horse can cause more harm than gymnastic improvement.

2. Horsemanship is not merely a matter of bodily skills, but is based on scholarship and, therefore, is a matter of the mind and intellect. Good horsemanship is based on proper character development and, therefore, is also a matter of mentality and spirit. Without the correct attitudes and insights, there cannot be the right sport.

3. Classical horsemanship is based on the scientific, gradual, systematic, natural and kindly development of the horse's natural potential to its utmost. That tradition is based on the love of the horse, and it emphasizes rewarding to teach and reinforce, and insists on teaching how to do right than punishing only what is misunderstood.

4. The reward of good horsemanship is nothing more or less than the contentment of the horse. Contentment is not only a matter of his state of mind, but also represents physical painlessness and comfort.

5. Lessons which are highly individualized to properly address the needs of the rider and the horse logically reveal good instruction.

6. Where knowledge terminates, brutality begins. Any brutality and compulsion against the horse reveals ignorance and bespeaks incorrect instruction.

7. Good training *asks* horses to give performance and teaches how best to deliver the desired performance. Horses should never be subjected to extortion and compulsion. Tyranny and terror have no place in equestrian life. Neither do force, pain or artifice.

8. An expert will pursue the truth about the horse's state of mind and athletic development rather than teach skills to cover up falsehoods and shortcomings.

14
One-Liners

Regarding the rider:

The job of the hands is to create longitudinal flexion by yielding.

Drive in the rhythm of the horse's footfalls.

The preparation of aids is more difficult than the delivery of aids, that is, *finesse*.

A person who manipulates with the hands alone is a rider in trouble.

If you can't discipline your own body, you cannot discipline your horse.

The horse knows how to be a horse......you have to learn to be a rider.

A rider is not a rubber band that stretches when the horse pulls on him.

Without elbows there is no riding.

The rider is the custodian of the tempo.

Good riding is distinguishable from bad riding because in good riding there is nothing you can see.

You can't correct a 2-track movement by doing a 2-track movement.

Less is more.

All breakthroughs come from riding forward.

Where knowledge ends, brutality begins.

The rider must be strong on himself and gentle to the horse.

The upper arms and elbows belong to the rider. The lower arms, and wrists belong to the horse.

Keep the elbows back so the horse can feel where you sit.

The hands should never inhibit the freedom of movement of the limbs.

Control comes from the depth of the seat.

To sit, lower your back softly and let the horse pull you down.

Work the seat down in all transitions.

The sensation of weightlessness is a thrilling consequence of correct riding.

Enter *into* the horse's movement rather than traveling *on it.*

Effortless riding comes with rhythm and balance.

The rider's silence comes from being quiet relative to the horse's motion.

When you post, do not stand up, "kneel up".

The stirrup is a small shelf on which you gently rest your toes.

When competing, ride the horse, not the test.

Regarding the horse:

The round top line is a prerequisite of impulsion.

Engagement is conditional on the horse being through in the neck and back.

The horse doesn't live in his head, he lives in his haunches.

The head must hang like a chandelier from the neck.

From the horse's point of view there are no statistics, only memory, so always work him correctly.

Speed is the enemy of impulsion.

The shoulder-in is the foundation of all two track exercises.

Never teach a horse *what not* to do, teach a horse *what* to do.

We never punish horses, we allow them to punish themselves.

You must create energy first in order to be able to collect it.

You don't get suspension until there is consistent rhythm.

The rider should aim to be the custodian of the horse's energy.

Not all flexed horses swing their backs.

Horses that make correct transitions do swing their backs.

You cannot drive the trot until the front end and the back end are united.

If the walk is aided a lot, it usually becomes inferior.

By always collecting the walk, you ruin it.

Through collection develops extension, and extension strengthens collection.

After the collection, comes the extension.

Disciplined riding is inspired by the horse because he trusts his education.

It's all right to look good if the riding has substance.

Always correct the horse by riding it forward.

You cannot shape a horse, only his energies.

The first energy you create in the horse should produce his posture also known as flexion and only the surplus energy beyond that can be spent for transportation.

There is no neutrality in riding: you are either actively improving your horse, or actively breaking him down.

The horse knows no right from wrong and learns everything indiscriminately. Therefore, in schooling him there is no neutrality.

The horse must carry his neck according to the flexibility and weight bearing capacity of the haunches.

Speed is the enemy of impulsion. Impulsion is manifested by the increased articulation of the joints of the hind legs, displayed by slow yet animated motion.

Horses should be anchored on their haunches and should not dwell on theirforehand. The success of this depends on the development of lumbar tucking of the pelvis forward and under. The lumbo-sacral joint should flex and the hips need to be supple.

15
Conclusions

Now that you take leave of this book, I bid you to stay dedicated to the art of riding.

There are reasons for believing that horsemanship, practiced correctly, is an art. Everything based on scholarship that also has a spiritually uplifting dimension, we usually call art. Hence the expression, "the art of medicine." While horsemanship is incidentally also a sport because the communications between horse and rider are based on skilled tactual signals and physical prowess, it is not merely a sport.

Indeed, horsemanship has spiritually, or if you prefer, emotionally or mentally redeeming values. When it is practiced right, horsemanship makes for a beautiful display.

Let us make an imaginary journey among various aesthetic arts or categories of the "belle arti." Painting wants to depict a three dimensional physical reality and convey it beautifully on a two dimensional plane. Painting on a flat surface, the artist attempts to convey that the event depicted takes place in a three dimensional space. Those subjects that are acting in a painting convey the illusion that their actions take place in three dimensional reality. On a flat canvas one could certainly not wage battle or attend a school in Athens. Sculpture shows three dimensionally. One may walk around a piece of sculpture and realistically experience its relationship to surrounding space. However, its action remains illusion as it is frozen in space and time and only the human imagination can give it reality and "motion" with insight. Investing a statue with life one arrives at the art of dancing and gymnastics. The former is the stronger messenger of imagination, the latter thrills more by its sheer vitality, daring and strength. Both these art forms are, in a way, statues in motion. For you may freeze any of their dynamic moments on a still photograph and you would get an image of a statue or a painting, both devoid of animation, yet still invested with beauty. The art of riding advances the dimensions of experienced reality, yet further than dancing and gymnastics. The new sophistication equestrian arts bring is to foster beauty and harmony in motion of two utterly unlikely partners. United in dance-like harmony are two creatures in a right angled interception, utterly unlike in size, strength, power, temperament and intentions. While the differences are enormous between the participating species, the communication areas are minuscule and the partner's customary sensory and emotional awareness are vastly different. The horse is "nature lived through instincts." This is different from people, who conduct themselves mostly by the guidance of their emotions. Not to imply that horses can understand rationality, but we know also that humans seldom act rationally either. For a horse to even imagine the nature of human emotionality as the basis of behavior is as unimaginable as for us are those things in the universe we label "mysteries." Nothing is similar between horse and rider. The art of the rider is to cajole his benign partner into harmoniously shared action. The visual

The artistic liberty that forces the legs forward and the toes down are forgivable in light of the heroic elevation this gives to the flag. The cadenced and collected horse tells how well his rider balanced herself with a flag. Doing a man's job in battle, Jeanne d'Arc dressed and rode like one. The legendary heroine of France would have not seen glories without the horse, nor would she be properly revered now without being seated on one whose cadence she mastered.

consequences include immense visual beauty the likes of which one can never notice in a human unless he is enthroned on a horse. Equally, the horse becomes an artistic monument to the Baroque ideal of random nature made glorious by human intellect. The shaping and honing of the horse's natural beauty and energies, in the custody of an inspired equestrian, will not only preserve what nature bequeathed to the horse but glorify it in splendor. Thus the added artistic dimension is the unity of unlike creatures resolved in harmony born of mutual pleasure.

In the equestrian art, beyond aesthetic beauty one finds an attractive inspirational, perhaps spiritual beauty. This beauty is born of the possibility that the human intellect can animate the horse and command the horse's entire attention. Free as the wind, wild and powerful in nature, the horse now surrenders his will to his rider's intellect. More than intellect, insight and skills, the rider desolves in feelings and reveals his emotions through his art in commanding his horse. For when we ride, we are more visible to others than during other endeavors. When we ride, our emotions are manifested as dynamic images and actions.

And so it transpires that if the "beautiful arts" (belle arti) can be measured by their sophistication in the number of dimensions their experience contains, the riding of horses maybe the greatest art of them all. For it contains dimensions of sophisticated experiences surpassing the nearest of kin, dancing and gymnastics.

Realizing the merits of the equestrian arts, the traditional leading classes of Western society made sure that their young elite received an education on horseback. For horses can educate through first hand, subjective, personal experiences, unlike human tutors, teachers and professors can ever do. Horses can build character, not merely urge one to improve on it. Horses forge the mind, the character, the emotions and inner lives of humans. People can talk to one another about all these things and remain distanced and lonesome. In the partnership with a horse, one is seldom lacking for thought, emotion and inspiration. One is always attended by a great companion.